party planning secrets

THE ULTIMATE GUIDE TO A SUCCESSFUL PARTY

CHARLIE SCOLA aka **PARTYCHARLIE**
with **KATTI LIPPA**

Party Planning Secrets
The Ultimate Guide to a Successful Party
by Charlie Scola

Published by: Clear Toast Publications
                 17226 Grevillea Avenue, Suite I
                 Lawndale, CA 90260
                 E-mail: info@PartyCharlie.com
                 Website: www.PartyCharlie.com

Library of Congress Control Number: 2007900655

ISBN-13: 978-0-9791878-0-3
ISBN-10: 0-9791878-0-X

Printed in the United States of America

0 9 8 7 6 5 4 3 2 1

DISCLAIMER
As a professional party planner and caterer for over 30 years, I have given you information that will be very helpful, but every crowd and situation is different and planning may differ from party to party.

The PartyCharlie cartoon was created by Gary Tharler.
All other artwork is by Gramy Maksrivorawan.

Editing by Barri Sturm and Lois Smith
Page Design by Carolyn Porter
    One-on-One Book Production, West Hills, California
Cover by Todd Meisler of ZD Design and Barri Sturm
Production: Nancy Gadney

Napkin-folding examples, pages 291-300, are used with permission of Republic Master Chefs Textile Rental Services (www.Republic MasterChefs.com), copyright © 1998 by Milliken & Company.

 Please recycle at home and at your parties.

Table of Contents

Section 2. PLANNING YOUR PARTY

In Loving Memory

To my grandmother,
"Mama."

An amazing woman
and a great cook.

We love and miss you, Mama.

This book is dedicated in loving memory to my grandmother, "Mama" — an amazing woman who was born in 1909 and lived a vibrant life until 2005. Mama always loved to laugh. She was one of the world's best cooks. When I was a child, I remember running home because Mama was cooking one of my favorite dishes. (Well, to tell you the truth, every dish of hers was my favorite.) She loved everyone, and everyone loved her. I spoke at her funeral to a packed room of friends and relatives. I told everyone, "Go and love each other as Mama loved you." After I said that, I realized those very words were similar to the words that Jesus Christ spoke. I'm sure Mama's cooking for Jesus. If you're lucky enough to get into Heaven, just ask anyone up there where Mama's kitchen is. Oh — and bring an appetite!

We love you and miss you, Mama!

Foreword

$\mathcal{I}$n today's hectic world, we need to take advantage of every excuse to have a party. Partying, celebrating, and socializing releases positive energy and reminds us of who we are as human beings. Parties and celebrations help to bring us together so we can celebrate life and one another. Celebrating with one another reignites our sense of community. We are one country, one world, one people. Join me in making it a better world one party at a time.

There are actual health benefits to making or attending parties. Several universities have published reports with mounting evidence that an active social life may help people to lead better, longer lives. Scientific research and physical evidence show that socializing boosts the immune system, which is the body's first line of defense against disease. Researchers have stated that the benefits of celebrating at parties far outweigh the caloric effects of occasionally eating more food during a gathering.

Celebrating together also brings mental health benefits, including positive thinking. Scientists have proposed that socializing activates a system in the brain that releases natural opiates. These opiates have a calming effect, creating a sense of well-being. Psychologists believe that positive thinking will enable you to live a happier, healthier life. A recent landmark study even suggests that celebrating and socializing help to fill emotional gaps. The scientists conducting this study have produced evidence that socializing can reduce the kind of tension and stress most of us experience on a daily basis. In fact, the results

were so significant, the researchers concluded, that not socializing is as detrimental to your health as smoking or being overweight.

History shows how important parties and celebrating are to people in all cultures. Consider that every religion has a form of celebration — for instance, the first Thanksgiving in America in 1621. This harvest celebration has become a mainstay in American society, and as the name suggests, it is a special opportunity for us to give thanks for the bounty in our lives. Then there's Independence Day, the fourth of July. On July 4, 1776, America claimed its independence, and for every year after that, we've been celebrating our personal independence with food, fun, and fireworks. And who could forget New Year's Eve? This special day has been recognized for hundreds of years, but since the 1900s, New Year's Eve has been an occasion to celebrate and make personal life-changing resolutions. Anniversaries are celebrated by people, companies, institutions, and governments. And of course there is the marriage celebration.

No matter what the purpose of the party or celebration, the effects are the same: A party or celebration promotes community, improved mental and physical health, and a renewed sense of self. At a good party or celebration, we can feel as if time has stopped, and the only things that seem important are being with those we care about and sharing the best of ourselves.

> *"Remember to LOVE, because that's how we got here and that's how we'll stay here."*
> — **Charlie Scola**

Introduction

*T*hink about the last time you decided to have a party. Usually party planning starts with all the right intentions. You decide which foods to cook and which guests to invite. You feel a burst of energy. Parties are fun — just the word *party* conjures up some of your most creative ideas. That's what I call the creative energy flow, and it's a great feeling. But it can come to a screeching halt and become a chore which creates overwhelming stress when you realize there are many components of a party.

Avoid the stress and realize the energy with some simple planning tools. Let me tell you about the Five P's.

Perfect Planning Prevents Poor Performance

In this book you'll find advice and hands-on learning derived from years and years of my professional experiences condensed into easy-to-read suggestions and answers to questions that authors of most books about party planning never thought to address.

Creating a party is like building a house. You start with the idea, then you need the blueprints (planning), then you start building room by room (the guest list, menu, entertainment, decorations, etc.). With the information in this book and the templates for planning your event, inter-

viewing vendors, scheduling staff or volunteers, designing your buffet or potluck, and knowing the quantities of food and beverage, your party will be a giant success.

Creating the Energy and Keeping It Flowing

Have you noticed that some parties seem to be just a gathering of people, while other parties seem to have a life of their own and are full of exciting energy? Sometimes that energy happens on its own, sometimes it's the mix of people, sometimes it's the time of year, and sometimes it's the music. How do you know your party will be successful? Do you just hope you'll have all the right elements and everything will fall into place? If you do, you'll be taking a big chance.

Throughout this book I talk about generating energy and keeping it flowing. You can ensure that your party will be a big hit by planning not just for success — but for **outrageous success!** How? Just read on and follow PartyCharlie's Five Steps to 'Create the Energy' for an Outrageously Exciting Party. In addition to all the usual details of planning a great party — all covered in this book — there's a formula for achieving that energy. It's not complex, and we all can do it.

Why I Wrote This Book

In your many experiences in life, you may have noticed how good it feels when you've shared some gem of information that you know will really help someone else. In my life, I've noticed this as well. And with that in mind, I have expanded my horizon in catering by teaching people how to produce their own **perfect party**. As much as I would like to plan and cater the parties of every person reading this book, I can't be everywhere at once.

Party Planning Secrets

So, by offering professional industry tips and sharing my step-by-step methods, I can help you create every detail of your party, whether it's for work, family and friends, charity events, political dignitaries, or even celebrities. My goal is to take the mystery out of planning and preparing any type of party and to eliminate any pre-party stress and anxiety you may have experienced in the past. I want to help you create **and enjoy** the perfect party.

For years, friends and clients have called me and said things like, "Charlie, we're having a small gathering, and we're going to do it ourselves. I just have a quick question if you wouldn't mind answering it." And I would answer the question, whether it was about buffet decorating or food preparation or dealing with vendors, and I'd be happy and honored that they called. The way I saw it, if they're doing a party themselves, then they're not using anybody else to cater it — so they're not cheating on me! But the idea that they would take time to call made me feel good and made me realize that I do have some authority on the subject.

Over the years, I realized that a lot of people don't know this information and that compiling it in one resource would be really helpful to them. You see, folks, I'm a caterer. Just the very nature of being a caterer explains my personality: A caterer caters. My job, whether it's planning a party or writing this book, is to provide, supply, accommodate, and gratify — *to cater*.

After years of being in the homes of clients from all walks of life, I've learned to develop shortcuts that make sense. These shortcuts maintain the quality but remove the stress. In my business, a good shortcut makes it easier for me as the caterer so that I can pass on the quality and

avoid tuckering out all the servers by the end of the event. These are the same tips I'll be teaching you in this book.

In addition, I've incorporated my answers to all those questions I've been asked over the years, as well as responses to a survey I sent out to clients asking them, "What would you most want to know to help you plan your own parties?" And I've made the instructions so easy to follow that even though it's always helpful to have a staff or volunteers, you *will* be able to handle the details on your own. If you do have a staff or volunteers, I'll help you to make the most of them.

I wrote this book so that it can be used as a tool for anyone and everyone throwing a party. If you're having a family get-together or holiday or birthday party, if you're planning a wedding, if you're involved in some type of charity group, if you're a human resources director who wants to stay within a small budget for the next office gathering, if you're a restaurant owner who is thinking of getting involved in the catering business in order to enhance your revenue, if you're an entrepreneur looking to enter the big-dollar business of party planning and catering, or if you're having a party just for the fun of it — this book is for you. Here you'll find helpful tools, whether you know your way around the kitchen or you don't have a clue but are prepared to give it a go. Either way, consider me your personal tour guide.

By the time you reach the last page, you'll be more confident talking to vendors, and have an edge to prevent embarrassing party moments. If you're a restaurant owner or entrepreneur, you'll find ways to increase sales by providing amazing services at a low cost.

In short, this book will show you how to make the most of your time, money, and efforts to enjoy the process and have a fun, fabulous party.

The PartyCharlie Website

Please visit my website at www.partycharlie.com for wonderful party products delivered right to your door! For decorations, disposable ware, flowers, new and exciting updated fun cutting-edge party ideas, the newest food trends and more!

Sign up for my **free** monthly newsletter. Receive **free** gifts and enter my contests to win fun prizes.

How to Use This Book

In order to make the most of every page in this book, I've designed it to be easy to understand and use. It's divided into seven sections:

Section 1: "PartyCharlie's Philosophy" describes my personal, proven philosophy about what it takes to create a fun and fabulous event.

Section 2: "Planning Your Party" helps you keep the overall picture in mind, guiding you through the party basics, such as choosing a date, planning a theme, and creating invitations.

Section 3: "Presentation: Putting It All Together" takes you step by step through every possible detail once you've decided to have a party. From making space to finding a florist, I'll answer some questions you may have always had and some questions you might not have even thought to ask.

It also includes *The PartyCharlie 1-2-3 Step,* which will help guide you in setting up the food on your buffet.

Section 4: "The Small Details That Make a Big Impact" includes more than two dozen ways to involve your guests, how to use volunteers, and tips on offering your own or hired coat check.

Section 5: "The Day of Your Party" will help you make sure things run smoothly as all those details come together, as well as handle some of the unexpected elements, like the guest who doesn't want to (or can't) leave.

Section 6: "After Your Party" will help reduce the drudgery of cleanup.

Section 7: "Vendors and Rentals" covers a wealth of information, tips, and cautions to help you find the right services and make sure they're doing everything as you planned.

Although this is not a cookbook (if you need one, check out my upcoming *PartyCharlie Shouts "Quit Running In and Out of the Kitchen": Menus That Are Designed to Keep You in the Party and Not in the Kitchen),* you'll find concise tips and suggestions in bulleted form so that even if you're reading the book days before your party, you'll find what you need summarized clearly and simply. Certain information is repeated in various sections throughout the book because I realize that, as with any reference book, you may not read it cover to cover.

Party Planning Secrets

In party planning, as in life, mistakes are made. I've made them all! And through experience, I've learned how to avoid them. This book will help you do things right the first time. Yes, you'll be learning a new skill. Yes, sometimes that can be intimidating. But with *Party Planning Secrets*, your party planning will be made easy. Just think of how many things you've dealt with in your life that were harder than throwing a successful party. Every challenge probably helped to make you stronger, to broaden your skills. With my help and this book, you **can** throw the perfect party.

Section 1

PARTYCHARLIE'S PHILOSOPHY

Chapter 1

Party, Celebrate, and Socialize Your Way to Health and Success

*W*hat does the word *party* mean, anyway? It has received an undeserved bad rap. Let's start with Webster's definition:

Party: A gathering for social entertainment or the entertainment itself, often of a specific nature; as, a card party, or cocktail party.

Now let me give you <u>my</u> definition:

Party: When two or more people gather to lift each other's spirits and celebrate life.

Throughout all my research, nowhere have I read that downing a fifth of booze and getting incoherent is the definition of a party. Of course, it's possible to achieve that objective at a party if you so desire. However, it's definitely not the route to partying, celebrating, and socializing your way to health and success.

So, how is it possible to party, celebrate, and socialize your way to health and success? I write a column for several newspapers under my pen name, Charlie Scola aka Party Charlie. When I wrote the article, "Party, Celebrate, and Socialize Your Way to Health and Success," I received countless e-mails from readers praising me for the article and wanting to know more. I couldn't believe how many people felt this message needs to be expanded upon. So here we go.

I've witnessed the health and success benefits of partying all around me. So, if you're feeling guilty for feeding your face a bit too much at a party or at holiday season, I have good news for you. Partying, celebrating, and socializing is a healthy way of life. Take a look at any successful individual, and most likely he or she is socially outgoing and enjoys a good party.

Yes, socializing is very beneficial to your health. Here's why. Mental health practitioners have been telling us for years to get out and socialize. Partying, celebrating, and socializing is a way to boost your immune system. And, with so much talk today about threats to our immune system, we need all the help we can get. Social contact in a friendly, pleasant, upbeat environment is extremely reinforcing to who we are. By nature, we are social creatures and, therefore, socializing and partying enriches us. So, why are some of us not participating? Here are some of the reasons: "I'm too old." "I'm not hip enough." "I'm too tired." "I don't have the time." "It's too far." "I don't like the food they're serving." "My clothes don't fit." "I'm shy." Go ahead and add your excuse to the list, but if you want some long-overdue happiness, start joining the party.

Here's more good news: happier people live longer. Elaine Wethington, Associate Professor, Department of Human Development and Department of Sociology, Cornell University and co-director of the Bronfenbrenner Life Course Center, states that people who have a strong social support system have a greater sense of well-being. Lisa Berkman, *Thomas Cabot Professor* of Public Policy and the Harvard School of Public Health, and chair of the school's Department of Society, Human Development and Health says, "studies have shown that people who are socially isolated or 'disconnected' from others are at increased risk for poor health and dying." I'm not making this up. So, you can make your excuses or, you can jump into the game of life.

Meeting people at a social event is good for your professional life. I frequently see and hear party guests exchanging numbers and talking about meeting again to explore a possible business relationship. Meeting someone at a social event automatically validates you because you're on the guest list. Even if you're a guest of a guest, it still brings you into the circle. People feel a sense of comfort because you're all at the same place for the same reason — to celebrate something specific.

Want to be a kind neighbor? If you know someone who's a little down and lonely, next time you're invited to a party, do them a life-changing favor — invite them! And if you yourself enjoy a good party, all I have to say is — Party On! For those of you who have been missing out on wonderful parties, try this the next time when someone says, "We're having a party, can you make it?" Think first, and then say with a smile, "I would be honored to attend your party." Who knows, maybe PartyCharlie will be catering it!

Chapter 2

Creating the Energy

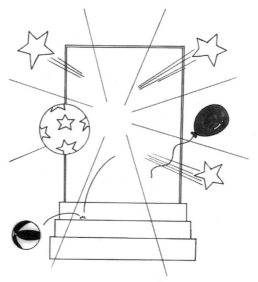

$\mathcal{H}$ave you ever noticed the energy flow at award shows like the Oscar's and Grammy's or at the entrance of a cruise ship before the *bon voyage*? That kind of energy would never exist to the degree that it does if the people who plan the events did not create it.

You may not know this, but there is a formula for creating that energy. It is really very simple. However, as simple as the formula may be, in order to achieve the maximum effect, it must proceed in the right order. As with any recipe or formula, the order, amount, and timing must be in sync. I have stumbled onto this process both consciously and subconsciously. You see, all my life I have enjoyed the energy that comes from people who are partying, celebrating, and socializing. When guests enter a party, I have observed the change that appears in them immediately upon their being greeted, welcomed, and acknowledged. In my younger days as a banquet manager maître d', just being in the presence of that energy was so powerful that sometimes it was impossible to get to sleep at night. Today, I feel blessed by the energy I receive from the people I meet at the many affairs I plan and cater.

The Great Party Myth

So, what creates a great party? Many people think that great food and great music make a great party, and I agree. These are each important components of a great party. But it's not just great food and music that make a great party. As you will read in my next chapter, "Five Steps to 'Create the Energy' for an Outrageously Exciting Party," great food and music are only two of the Five Steps needed. Through my speaking engagements, I have been offered an eclectic list of what others think make an outrageously exciting party. Each one is an essential element of an outrageously exciting party, but you will see what an amazing party you can create when you include all the elements of my Five Steps.

Lots of people think a good party is because of the *people*. Yes, your guests play a big part in a great party. However, you can't expect everyone to walk in and have high energy and a good time just because they're there.

Other people think a good party is because of the *location*. Yes, if your location is beautiful, wonderful, and interesting, your guests will enjoy the ambiance. But your location alone will not create the energy for an exciting party.

I've also had people tell me they think it's the *food* that makes a great party. Again, great food and beverages are important. But in all my years of catering and party planning, I have never seen anyone get up and boogie because the prime rib was juicy! It's not the food alone. We eat every day, and some of us indulge quite well.

One person told me that in the *invitation*, you should tell your guests to come happy or don't come at all. That might not be such a bad idea. However, if you don't follow through once your guests arrive, your party will definitely not be as exciting as you or your guests expected.

As you will see in the next chapter, creating the energy is a combination of my Five Steps to an Outrageously Exciting Party. Enjoy the process of lifting your guests' spirits and getting them excited, and watch the magic happen.

Chapter 3

Five Steps to 'Create the Energy' for an Outrageously Exciting Party

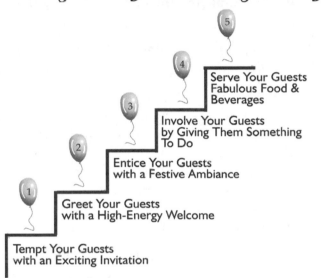

5

4 — Serve Your Guests Fabulous Food & Beverages

3 — Involve Your Guests by Giving Them Something To Do

2 — Entice Your Guests with a Festive Ambiance

1 — Greet Your Guests with a High-Energy Welcome

Tempt Your Guests with an Exciting Invitation

*G*et ready to have fun while you learn how to make it happen. Once you learn my Five Steps, everyone you know will be coming to you for your great tips! So help them out and spread the joy of partying, celebrating, and socializing your way to health and success.

Before beginning the Five Steps, you need to choose a date for your party. Look closely at your calendar to make sure you're not planning your party or event in conflict with a holiday, awards show, major sporting event, three-day holiday weekend, or any special events in your

community — unless, of course, your event is tied to that particular holiday or event.

Also, be aware of Daylight Saving Time. People will usually arrive early or show up late depending on whether the time is springing ahead or falling back.

See Chapter 9, "Date and Time – The Best Choice for Your Party" for more information on choosing the right date.

STEP #1: *Tempt Your Guests with an Exciting Invitation*

Once you've selected your date, it's time for the invitation. This is where the energy begins. You can begin by sending out "save the date" notices or just get the buzz going by word of mouth. When writing your invitation, make sure to include all the details and use high-energy words that convey positive and motivating energy. Below is an example of two invitations. You decide which of the two parties you'd rather attend based on the invitation:

> **Example 1:** It's Joey's Birthday! Come join us Saturday, July 12th at Noon for a Birthday BBQ and Pool Party. 1234 Old Oak Road (555) 444-1234. Please RSVP by July 1st.

> **Example 2:** It's Joey's 4th Birthday! Saturday, July 12th at high noon. Come and join the celebration! Swimming, Barbequing the Best Ribs in Town and Serving a Big Yummy Birthday Cake. Bring your favorite beverage and don't forget your swim trunks. We'll have all the rest of the goodies. 1234 Old Oak Road (555) 444-1234. Please RSVP by July 1st.

The first invitation leaves out important information that people need to know, such as what to wear and what to bring. It definitely doesn't convey much excitement — there are no high-energy words. However, the second invitation includes all the necessary information and delivers an exciting and tempting message.

Remember, as important as it is to create energy with the invitation, it's equally important to include all the facts, such as the date, time, directions, and RSVP information. Read more about invitations in Chapter 13, "Invitations — How to Invite Your Guests."

STEP #2: *Greet your Guests with a High-Energy Welcome*

Folks, this step works like magic! The positive energy flow starts when a friendly greeter personally welcomes everyone entering the party.

Here's a situation I'm sure many of you can relate to. You arrive at a nice restaurant, and the hostess is on the telephone. There is no acknowledgment from the hostess that you've arrived. You feel uneasy while waiting for some sign of recognition from the hostess who is still on the phone. Your uneasiness builds as you wait. After hanging up the phone and writing the reservation in the book, she finally greets you, takes you to your table, and says, "Enjoy your meal." Chances are you're not beginning your dining experience on a very good note.

Here's how you should have been treated. Upon entering the restaurant, the hostess excuses herself from the telephone for a moment to acknowledge you with a big smile, letting you know she'll be right with you. Once off

the phone, she cheerfully welcomes you, thanks you for your patience, and shows you to your table.

Think about how you may have felt in each scenario. I'm sure you'd be much happier being treated in the second scenario than in the first.

Now imagine a similar situation at a party. The door is open or you ring the bell, and someone who just happens to be near the door opens it and says, "Come on in." You ask for the hosts, and the guest replies, "I don't know, I haven't seen them." You enter and people are mingling. You wander around looking for some acknowledgment. Other guests glance over and give you a small smile; remember, they entered the same way and are just getting comfortable themselves.

Do you feel welcomed and acknowledged? I doubt it. The way you're greeted at the entrance kick-starts your energy. It gives you a sense of belonging that makes you feel welcomed. By the way, for those of you who are familiar with Dr. Abraham Maslow's hierarchy of fundamental human needs, the third most important one is a sense of belonging.

Make your guests feel welcomed as soon as they arrive.

Welcome your guests at the door. If you can't be at the door, have someone else greet your guests. Choose a close friend or someone with an upbeat attitude. As a host, you should always introduce guests to each other. As I mentioned above, a warm welcome puts people at ease and gives them a sense of belonging. It's all about creating that positive energy flow.

Here's an example of a greeting that you or your greeter can use to pass along that upbeat, positive energy:

"Hi, my name is PartyCharlie. Rose and Ray are out back where hors d'oeuvres are being served. The bar is to your left, and the DJ is taking requests. Have a wonderful time and let me know if there's anything you need."

Some hosts like to decorate the entrance of their party. If you have the budget or resources, by all means decorate it. The more welcoming and inviting, the better. If you're having a themed party, include the theme in your entrance. Have your decorations and greeters match the theme. Your entrance doesn't have to be elaborate to be inviting. A simple welcome banner and balloons are always festive.

STEP #3: *Entice Your Guests with a Festive Ambiance*

Continue to build your party's energy level by creating a fun and festive ambiance. You don't have to spend a bundle. Simply changing the lighting in your home will make a big difference. Soft lighting changes the mood dramatically. Pink light bulbs give the room a warm glow. Just make sure your food and beverage areas are well lit.

Continue the theme from your entrance throughout your party. Whether you choose balloons and streamers or more elaborate decorations, place them throughout the party. This lets your guests know you took the time to make it a special event.

Music is also important to get energy flowing at your party. Make sure your music is not playing at maximum level as your guests arrive. Allow some time for each of your guests to get acquainted and into the party spirit. Then you can raise the volume gradually as the party progresses.

Rearrange your furniture to accommodate the party. Remember, your home is set up for everyday living, not a party. Move the furniture to the garage or to the side of the rooms to create a mingling area. Just because you have the room doesn't mean you need to use all of it — don't spread the party out too much . When you spread the party all over the place, you lose the energy. Keep the space comfortable.

Dancing — yeah, baby! Get your guests dancing by creating a dance area. When you set aside an area specifically for dancing, people will use it. The dance area shouldn't be so large that it's intimidating. People will join the dancing if the dance floor is crowded. Don't worry — people will dance on the perimeter of the dance floor, whether it's grass, carpet, or concrete.

STEP #4: *Involve Your Guests by Giving Them Something to Do*

Give your guests opportunities to participate in the festivities. Have games, quizzes, or giveaway prizes for the best costume or best dancer. One of my favorite ways of creating participation is through a murder mystery.

It doesn't really matter what you choose as long as it's fun and easy. Most people will get involved if you make games and activities available for them while others enjoy watching and cheering for the winners. Engaging your guests helps keep the energy of your party going.

Read more about "Guests – Getting Them Involved" in Chapter 32.

STEP #5: *Serve Your Guests Fabulous Food and Beverages*

Food and beverages are as important as any of the other four steps. Some of you may feel that food makes the party. It's true that great food gets great reviews. However, a simple BBQ or buffet with chicken can be just as rewarding as a full-course gourmet meal. People remember the experience of the party, not just the food. They'll talk about how good the food was because they were having a good time. I've been at parties where lobster and caviar were served, but I couldn't wait to make a break for the door. Folks, food is important, but as I said before, no one gets up and boogies because the prime rib was juicy.

Here are some tips to make your fifth step as successful as the previous four.

As you will read in the next chapter, "Know Your Crowd," when planning your party, it's important to consider your guests. What you like is important, but design your party — including your menu — around your guests. Here are a few ideas about how to make sure your food and beverages are fun and fabulous:

- Offer a variety of foods. Giving your guests choices is key to any great menu.

- Presentation is everything. Use a variety of colors and textures when creating your menu.

- Messy foods don't work when your crowd is dressed up.

- Match beverages to your food. Wine is a great choice for a party, and there are a variety of wines to go with any menu.

Now you have all Five Steps. Enjoy the thrill of hosting a party that everyone will talk about. Please visit me at *www.partycharlie.com* and click on Contact to let me know how your party went using these steps. I'm always happy to hear success stories. I know your next party will be the next success story. I look forward to hearing from you.

Don't Break Up the Energy of Your Party

Once you've followed my Five Steps and have created an outrageously exciting party, don't break up the energy flow just to keep to a perfect schedule. For example: A long time ago, when I was a banquet manager catering weddings, my duties were to schedule the events which included the bridal entrance, the first dance, and cutting of the cake. We were always on a time schedule. I remember times when it was time to cut the cake or make a toast, yet, the dance floor was packed with guests having a great time. I decided to delay the cake cutting or the toast so the guests could enjoy the energy in the room. Sure, I would have to make up that time elsewhere, but staying on a strict schedule is not the most important element of a good party; fun is the most important element of a good party.

I remember hearing from other party managers how perfectly on schedule their parties went. And I thought, "so what!" I can keep the party hopping by keeping the energy going. I never listened to those managers who thought keeping on schedule was the object of a good party. Instead, I made sure that the hosts and guests were happy, which was good for me, as well, because I always received huge smiles and great tips!

Chapter 4

Know Your Crowd

The key to all Five Steps is to *know your crowd*. Instead of planning your party around what *you* like, consider what your *guests* like. This goes for all stages of your party, such as your theme, music, and menu.

- Garlic is great, but if it's a cocktail party and people are talking close to each other, think twice about the amount you use.

- Consider the age group of your guests. This will tell you a little bit about their eating habits. Older people tend to stay away from spicy and chewy foods, whereas younger people like trendy foods.

- For a children's party with lots of adults in attendance, provide two menus: one for the children and one for the adults.

- Knowing your crowd will tell you if you should serve beer, wine, or possibly tropical blended drinks. Maybe it's a martini crowd.

- If it's a dancing crowd, make sure to provide music and an area for dancing.

Party Planning Secrets

⅄ Themes are great, but a toga party probably would not be a great choice for an older crowd. But then again, maybe it will. That's the point of knowing your crowd.

Take a minute and consider the crowd. It's that simple!

Section 2

PLANNING YOUR PARTY

Chapter 5

Budgeting and Planning Your Party

Creating a Budget

*a*n important — and often overlooked — element in planning a party is to establish an appropriate budget. When putting a budget together, keep in mind that there will always be last-minute, unanticipated costs, such as additional guests or sudden bad weather that calls for tenting and heaters.

Let's face it, you won't be able to plan for every little shortfall, but you can save money, time, and your sanity by using my Budget Worksheet as a guide when planning your event. (See Chapter 55, "PartyCharlie Templates and Checklists.")

The worksheet includes these categories:

- [ ] Event location
- [ ] Staff
- [ ] Food and beverages
- [ ] Invitations
- [ ] Disposable ware
- [ ] Rentals
- [ ] Entertainment
- [ ] Accessories
- [ ] Services
- [ ] Transportation
- [ ] Miscellaneous

I guarantee that if you complete my budget worksheet, you won't forget anything!

PartyCharlie's Party Checklist

The PartyCharlie Party Checklist in Chapter 55 is guaranteed to make your party a huge success while saving you lots of worry about getting lost in the details. It spells out exactly what you should do 6 to 8 weeks prior (budgeting, deciding on the type of party, location, time, etc.), 3 to 4 weeks before (including mailing the invitations, planning the menu, arranging to buy or rent furniture or decorations, lining up the vendors, and more), 1 to 2 weeks before (purchasing goods), the day or two prior (food prep, etc.), and, finally, the big day (including having fun!).

See Chapter 55, "PartyCharlie Templates and Checklists."

Chapter 6

Money – How to Save It and Tips on Getting Discounts

$\mathcal{H}$ere's the deal — money isn't funny, and you won't be laughing if you spend more than you have to. Use my book as a party-planning guide rather than hiring a party planner. Trust yourself. You *can* throw the PartyCharlie Perfect Party. Here are some general tips:

- Consider co-hosting your party with friends or relatives. A joint party takes some coordinating, but sharing in costs can really make it worthwhile.

- Consider the number of guests carefully. The enthusiasm of throwing a party coupled with wanting to make sure you have plenty of guests can make for a longer guest list and a greater expenditure than need be.

Party Planning Secrets

☐ The length of the party directly correlates with how much money you'll spend on food, beverages, disposable ware, and any staff/labor you may need. You don't need to have a party for six or seven hours. A typical party runs about four hours, weddings about five hours.

☐ Choose the day of your party wisely. Most services (including catering, venue and equipment rentals, and entertainment) usually cost more on Saturdays and during high-demand seasons. By avoiding the dates listed in Chapter 9, "Date and Time – The Best Choice for Your Party," you may be able to get better prices.

☐ Hold your event in the late afternoon or late evening. That way you can serve cocktails and hors d'oeuvres rather than a full meal. Remember, you'll need to indicate on your invitations that it's a cocktail and hors d'oeuvres party so guests are aware it's not a dinner party.

☐ Having an early afternoon event may include a full lunch, but you'll save money on beverages. Alcohol consumption is significantly lower during an afternoon event versus an evening event.

☐ Merchants pay a fee to process a credit card transaction. Ask rental companies and service providers for a discount if you pay in cash. Always get a receipt.

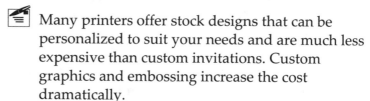

Saving Money on Invitations

Many printers offer stock designs that can be personalized to suit your needs and are much less expensive than custom invitations. Custom graphics and embossing increase the cost dramatically.

Engraving and letterpress are the most expensive printing options. Other, more economical printing methods include thermography (raised lettering that gives the illusion of engraving), flat printing, offset printing, laser printing, and lithography.

Use nonmetallic inks. Most companies charge a standard fee for black, gray, and colored inks. Inks with silver, gold, and bronze are more expensive.

Professional calligraphers are expensive. Ask a friend with beautiful handwriting to help you instead. Computer calligraphy is also an economical option.

Rather than having your stationer assemble your invitations, gather your friends to help you tie, stuff, and seal them at home. Use self-adhesive stamps and a sealer sponge or glue stick to seal the envelopes.

You should order 25 extra envelopes in the event of errors during addressing so you don't have to rush a small order to your door.

Hey, guess what – size **does** matter. I'm talking about invitations. Oversized invitations are interesting to look at, but they cost more to print

36

and mail. If you design your invitations to be extra long, extra wide, extra thick, extra heavy, or extra small, make sure you have the post office determine the proper postage before you have them printed.

Instead of including response cards (which cost more to print and mail), you can set up a website and/or e-mail address specific to your party. Most Internet providers allow you to have multiple e-mail addresses and space for a free personalized website. Your guests can RSVP from the website.

www.evite.com is also a great way to invite your guests. Some phone calls may be needed for non-computer users.

If your crowd is not likely to be Internet-savvy, for smaller parties, be sure to include your phone number on the invitation so guests can RSVP. Keep the guest list by the phone so you can mark it right away.

I invite you to my website, *www.partycharlie.com*, where you can shop online for fabulous party items, including invitations delivered right to your home or office.

Saving Money on Your Venue

If you're having a large party for which you need a venue other than your home, consider lower-cost alternative locations like local parks, community centers, church and synagogue social halls, lodges, or clubs, or call your local Chamber of Commerce for information about other venues.

 In terms of renting locations, Fridays and Sundays are usually less in demand than Saturdays. Some facilities will discount their rates on these days, so ask for the discount.

 Book your venue in advance. You can often avoid extra fees for booking early.

 If you're booking a venue at the last minute and the hall is available, ask for a special deal. The venue management would much rather have someone use the space than let it go empty.

Saving Money on Rentals and Disposable Ware

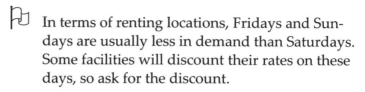 Consider using disposable plates and plastic tumblers rather than china and glassware. Some disposable ware now comes with stylish designs. It is less expensive to buy than glassware is to rent, and you don't have to worry about cleaning or breakage charges. For some parties, it's OK to mix plastic ware for food and glassware for beverage, or vice versa.

Go to *www.partycharlie.com* for offers on disposable ware shipped to your home.

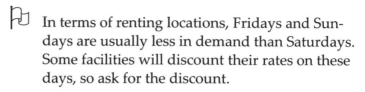 If you're renting equipment, dishware, or glassware, delegate someone to check each item before signing the delivery order. Unless you note the damaged or soiled pieces on the delivery ticket before you sign it, you will be charged when the goods are returned.

🍽 If you're renting plates, be sure to rinse them so they're free of food before you return them. Rental companies often charge a cleaning fee for dried-on food.

🍽 Avoid late charges by returning all rental items on time.

Saving Money on Food

🍽 Buffet-style service generally costs less than sit-down service. The labor cost alone for sit-down service (waiters and waitresses) is significant.

🍽 Provide appetizers at the tables or on a buffet rather than paying a server to tray-pass them. Of course, it's nicer to pass the hors d'oeuvres, but if you're on a budget, this is an area where you can save money. Ask a close friend or your kids to tray-pass — especially hot hors d'oeuvres.

🍽 Choose your entrée items wisely. A wonderful and inexpensive chicken dish can be just as appetizing as an expensive prime rib.

🍽 Themed or ethnic foods like Mexican or Italian with rice or pasta are generally less expensive.

🍽 Plan your menu with food items that are in season.

🍽 Plan a menu that has simple preparation steps. This will save you time, and if you're hiring food preparers, this will keep your staff cost down.

🍽 Look for sales on non-perishable items in advance. You may be able to save a lot on dry goods, beverages, and disposable items.

🍽 Consider your crowd when planning food quantities. A group of senior citizens will typically eat less than a group of graduating high school students. Men typically eat more than women.

🍽 Ask your guests to contribute a food item to the buffet. Potlucks can save a lot on food expenses. (See Chapter 18, "Potluck – Organizing a Successful Event.")

Saving Money on Beverages

🍸 Consider hosting only wine, beer, and soft drinks. The overall cost is lower than that for mixed drinks, unless you use high-cost wines.

🍸 Serve pitchers of sangria — it's inexpensive, festive, and flavorful.

🍸 Use proper glass sizes to avoid waste. If your glasses are too small, you'll find an increase in the number of drinks and cups consumed. If your glasses are too large, you'll find that there is a lot of waste because cold beverages get warm and are thrown away. A 10-ounce all-purpose plastic cup is a good size for mixed drinks, soft drinks, and even wine. Most beer drinkers prefer to drink from the bottle. If using keg beer, provide a 14-ounce cup.

Ⓨ Close the bar approximately 30 minutes before the end of the party and serve only soft drinks and coffee. This is not only good for saving money, but it also helps to ensure that your guests have time to sober up.

Saving Money on Floral Items

✃ Order your floral items far in advance. Be sure to ask what will be in season at that time.

✃ Avoid exotic flowers unless you can strike a deal with the florist.

✃ Avoid flowers that are in high demand for the season. For instance, roses are beautiful, but if your party is on or around Valentine's Day or Mother's Day, the cost will shoot up. (See Chapter 48, "Florists,"for additional ways to save money on floral items.)

Saving Money on Vendors

⚑ Research and book your caterer, entertainment, and any other vendors as soon as you know you'll need them.

⚑ When choosing vendors, use the "PartyCharlie Vendor Questionnaire." (See Chapter 55, "Party-Charlie's Templates and Guidelines.")

⚑ Big ads don't mean better service or prices, so shop around. Ask friends and co-workers for referrals.

Always get a second quote — remember to compare apples to apples.

Saving Money on Equipment

If you don't have it, borrow it. Ask your friends if they have some of the things you will need, such as chairs, tables, and coffeemakers.

Chapter 7

Safety — Making It a Priority

Using the Fire Extinguisher

Follow the fire department's "PASS system":

1. **P**ull the pin.

2. **A**im the extinguisher nozzle at the **base** of the flames.

3. **S**queeze the trigger while holding the extinguisher upright.

4. **S**weep the extinguisher from side to side, covering the area of the fire with the extinguishing agent.

NOTE: Be aware that fire extinguishers have different grades. For instance, a water-type extinguisher would spread a grease fire. A higher-grade extinguisher can douse most kinds of fires, whether it's a grease fire or a napkin that was accidentally set on the stove.

When renting or buying, be sure to check the class type:

Class type A extinguishers are for combustible materials such as paper, wood, cardboard, and most plastic.

Class type B fires involve flammable or combustible liquids such as gasoline, kerosene, grease, and oil.

Class type C fires involve electrical equipment, such as appliances, wiring, circuit breakers, and outlets. Never use water to extinguish class C fires — the risk of electrical shock is far too great!

Class type D fire extinguishers are usually found in a chemical laboratory. They are for fires that involve combustible metals, such as magnesium, titanium, potassium, and sodium.

PartyCharlie Safety Tips

☐ If you're using lights for design purposes — for instance, reflecting color lights off the walls — don't place bulbs near objects that can catch fire easily. The heat from a bulb can be intense.

☐ Always make sure the light fixtures are secured and won't tip over and burn the carpet or any other items.

☐ Make sure electrical/extension cords are firmly plugged in. Not doing so can cause sparks at the outlet.

☐ Tuck away or tape down cords so guests won't trip over them.

☐ Post emergency numbers next to the phone, including the local fire department, police department, and poison control center. We all know 911, but these days, you can't rely on 911 alone.

☐ Check that your smoke detectors are in working order.

☐ If you're having a large backyard party and expect people to be swimming in the pool, it's a good idea to have a lifeguard on hand. Some states have laws requiring that you have a lifeguard. Children must always be supervised. Also, only use plasticware around the pool. If someone breaks something in the pool, you may have to drain it!

- Keep watch over the self-service bar area to make sure no underage drinkers are serving themselves (or being served).

- Close the bar approximately 30 minutes before the end of the party and serve only water, soft drinks, and coffee so guests have a chance to sober up.

- Don't use anything breakable (such as a glass) to scoop out ice for your drinks. If the glass cracks without your noticing it, shards and splinters could end up in the drinks.

- Keep entrances and exits clear of clutter.

- Never put knives in a soapy sink. You may reach in later and…OUCH!

☐ Always clean and put knives away after you use them, even if you plan to use them again in the next few minutes.

☐ Never place a knife on the edge of your counter

☐ Keep floors dry and clean up spills immediately.

☐ When cooking, always keep pot handles turned in. This will prevent someone from knocking a pot off the stove or a child from touching it.

☐ Have a flashlight and first aid kit available. (See my First Aid Kit Supply Checklist in Chapter 55, "PartyCharlie's Templates and Checklists.")

Have fun & enjoy yourself! Remember, you're not launching the space shuttle — it's a party, and you should have fun creating wonderful energy!

Chapter 8

Electrical Power and Circuits —
Don't Overload Them

$\mathcal{K}$nowing your electrical needs and capacities is going to save you from having to deal with a power blowout in the middle of the party. By that time, the host or hostess might have had a couple of drinks, and it's a lot harder to handle power issues and work on the fuse box or circuit

breaker panel when you're a little tipsy. So prepare in advance to avoid a dangerous situation.

Safety Tips on Power and Circuits

As soon as you begin planning your party, start thinking about your power needs. Here are some ways of making sure you handle everything appropriately.

- Turn off appliances you won't be using for the party. Turn off air conditioning units in rooms that won't be used. Don't run big appliances from the same circuit. If it doesn't cause an overload, it can very well cause reduced power flow to the area where you need power (lights, DJ, coffeemakers).

- If you're planning to use a lot of extra electricity for your party, unplug your computer. Surge protectors work most of the time, but it's better to be safe.

- During the coffee-brewing process, don't make the mistake of plugging two coffeemakers into the same circuit, or you will most likely overload it. Once the coffee-brewing process is completed, it's OK to plug two coffeemakers into one plug because they draw about a quarter of the power when just keeping the coffee warm. If you don't have an extra circuit to spare, wait until one coffeemaker is finished brewing before starting the second one.

- Tuck away any wires from extra lamps, appliances, and band equipment. If they're in traffic areas, cover them with a throw rug or cord cover. Even duct tape can be used if that's all you have.

- Your circuits are broken up into amperage, and at the circuit breaker you'll be able to determine what capacity you have. Check your fuse box or breakers.

- A circuit generally carries 15 or 20 amps. If you're going to have a band, entertainment, or any vendor requiring power, ask the vender for power requirements. Some vendors may require a dedicated circuit.

- Consult a licensed and insured electrician if you're planning to use a lot of equipment, such as band equipment, lights, heaters, and coffeemakers.

- A licensed and insured electrician can temporarily pull power from your main breaker box and set up additional circuits. Costs range from $80 to $300 depending on the time it takes to do the work. Get a complete quote first!

- Check with your local rental companies to see if they have (quiet) power generators for rent. This might be a more appropriate and cost-efficient choice for your event.

- If you have questions, always follow the advice of a licensed, insured electrician. It's better to be safe than sorry.

Chapter 9

Date and Time — The Best Choice for Your Party

*S*o, you've decided to have a party. Congratulations on your birthday, anniversary, work accomplishment, or whatever the reason for your gathering. If you've hosted a party before, you may already know that there is something of an art to choosing the right time and date. For instance, a party that falls on Labor Day weekend may have low attendance because many people go out of town for the long weekend. Or if you have a party during the Final Four basketball tournament, your sports fan friends probably won't be there unless you happen to have large-screen TVs all around.

Choosing the Best Date and Time

☐ Take major holidays, local community functions, and sporting events into consideration. Even events that aren't a big deal to you personally might be a reason for your guests to stay home.

☐ Remember, you can have a party on any day of the week. You're likely to have less response on certain days, like Mondays, but it's not taboo.

☐ If you're planning a party for a weekday, keep in mind that most people will be coming directly from work. Choose a time early enough so they can scoot right over, have a good time, and then go home at a reasonable hour.

☐ For children or families, the best time for a party is Sunday afternoon. This gives them something to look forward to as a way of rounding out the weekend. Saturdays are a good second choice, but you'll find that some parents will still be working that day as well as attending their children's activities (soccer, baseball, etc.).

☐ For a party where alcohol is served, Saturday is a great night. Friday is a good backup night, but again, since more and more people are working on Saturdays, you may have a smaller turnout than if you wait until Saturday night.

☐ A party for adults will generally last four hours. It might last for five but tends to fizzle at that point. Knowing how long the party is going to last will be determined by how many activities you'll be having (gift opening, speeches, etc.), as well as whether you're serving several courses or just appetizers.

In general, a good time to start a dinner party is between 7:00 and 8:00 PM.

It might be a good idea to start a winter dinner party earlier than you would a summer dinner party because it gets dark earlier in the winter. Another reason is that if you live in an area of the country that has cold, snowy winters, you don't want people to have to drive home late at night when the roads are frozen.

If you're hosting a younger crowd, you may want to start later in the evening. For one thing, people like to arrive "fashionably late." For another, the earlier they arrive, the more liquor they'll likely be drinking, which means the more guests from whom you'll have to take away the keys. (And by the way, fashionably late is no longer fashionable — it's downright **rude**!)

If you're hosting an older crowd, as in a Golden Anniversary celebration, some of your guests might not want to stay up late. Consider having this kind of party early on a Saturday evening or on Sunday afternoon. Start it at 6:00 PM at the latest so that by 10:00 PM, your guests are out the door.

A children's party should last no more than three hours. Two and a half hours is optimum.

Daylight Saving Time, whether you're "falling back" or "springing ahead," often causes confusion. But if you must have the party on a day when the time is changing, include a reminder of the time change in your invitation.

Finally, below are some holidays and events that often prevent people from showing up at parties due to other obligations. Some events and religious holidays vary from year to year, so check your calendar.

List of Holidays and Events

January — New Year – January 1
Super Bowl – Last Sunday in January
or first Sunday in February

February — Academy Awards® – Varies
Mardi Gras – Always a Tuesday –
can vary from Feb. 3 - March 9
Olympics, Winter Games – Varies
Valentines Day – February 14

March —Daylight Saving Time – Second Sunday,
may vary (spring ahead at 2:00 A.M.)
Easter – Varies (March or April)
Final Four Basketball Tournament – Varies
Lent – 40-day period before Easter, Varies
Palm Sunday – Last Sunday of Lent,
Sunday before Easter (varies)
PartyCharlie's Birthday March 2 – Just kidding
Passover – Varies (March or April)
Purim – Varies
Stanley Cup – Varies

April — NBA Playoffs – Varies

May —High school prom – Varies (May or June)
Indy 500 – Varies
Kentucky Derby – Varies

    Memorial Day – Last Monday
    Mother's Day – Second Sunday

June—Father's Day – Third Sunday
    Graduation – Varies
    US Open (golf) – Varies
    Wimbledon (tennis) – Varies (June or July)

July —Family vacations
    Independence Day – July 4

August —Family vacations
    Olympics, Summer Games – Varies
    US Open (tennis) – Varies (August
    or September)

September — Labor Day – First Monday
    Rosh Hashanah, Yom Kippur – Varies
    (September or October)

October — Breeders Cup Championship – Varies
    Columbus Day – Second Monday
    Halloween – October 31
    World Series Final Game – Varies

November —Daylight Saving Time Over – First Sunday
    in November (may vary)
    Election Day – Tuesday on or after the 2nd
    Ramadan – Varies
    Thanksgiving – Fourth Thursday
    Veterans Day – November 11

December — Christmas – December 25
    Hanukkah – Varies
    Kwanzaa – Dec. 26 - Jan. 1
    New Year's Eve – December 31

Chapter 10

Theme – Selecting the Right One for Your Party

$\mathcal{C}$reating the energy with a theme can make the difference between an ordinary gathering and a spectacular event. A theme puts people in the mood and helps to keep your guests involved. Take, for instance, the ultimate theme party — a wedding reception. People are drawn in on every level. Everyone dresses a certain way. There's a time and area set aside for greeting the bride and groom. The single ladies gather to catch the bouquet, and the men

cheer at the removal of the bride's garter. People have something to do at every point and remain interested.

Giving your guests something to eat and turning on some music are only two of the Five Steps to creating the energy. Remember, we need all Five Steps! (See Chapter 3, "Five Steps to 'Create the Energy' for an Outrageously Exciting Party.")

Choosing the Right Theme

Choose something you personally like and enjoy for your theme. Any theme is a good theme as long as it fits your crowd. A 50th anniversary toga party might not go over so well, or depending on your guests, it might be a perfect fit.

Involve your guests — your theme can involve asking people to dress in costumes geared to the theme. You may feel as though you're ruffling a few of your guest's feathers by insisting on costumes, but when they show up in full regalia, they'll immediately be a part of what's going on. (See Chapter 32, "Guests – Getting Them Involved" for more tips.)

Costumes are fun and trendy. Visit my website, *www.PartyCharlie.com* or your local yellow pages for party costumes.

Add to a child's birthday by including a theme such as a favorite character or whatever is the latest trend among kids.

Party Planning Secrets

Purchase theme decor and products at a local party store or rent them from rental companies. Contact the local high school's or youth center's art department and ask if they can provide some fun props for the party.

Food and beverages should be used to enhance the theme of your party.

The cake can be a part of your theme as well. Cakes can be made in special shapes, like boats or cars. Any bakery can take your photograph and print edible pictures on icing sheets. Some can even "print" the photograph onto a type of sugar paper that can be placed on the cake.

Indicate that you're having a theme party on your invitations. Word your invitation to make it upbeat and exciting. (See Chapter 13, "Invitations – How to Invite Your Guests.")

Your party doesn't have to include costumes, props, or special lighting. In fact, if there's no particular reason for throwing your party, that can be a great theme too. The "just because" party can be an excellent reason to invite your friends to simply come and have fun. Remember to keep them entertained, and follow PartyCharlie's Five Steps to an Outrageously Exciting Party:

1. **Tempt Your Guests with an Exciting Invitation**
2. **Greet Your Guests with a High-Energy Welcome**
3. **Entice Your Guests with a Festive Ambiance**
4. **Involve Your Guests by Giving Them Something to Do**
5. **Serve Your Guests Fabulous Food and Beverages**

List of Themes

Art Deco	Jungle
African	Mad Hatter's Tea Party
Arabian	Mardi Gras
Asian	Mexican
Bavarian – Oktoberfest	Movie themes
The Beatles	Music: Roaring 20's, Rock &
Cars	Roll, Disco, Rap
Casino	Nautical
Celebrity lookalikes	Pajama party
Christmas	Patriotic
Christmas in July	Pet's birthday party
Circus	Pirates
Egyptian	Polynesian
Elvis	Renaissance
Fantasy	Seventies
Fifties	Sixties
French	Spanish
Futuristic	Sports
Greco-Roman	Toyland
Halloween	Twenties
Hawaiian luau	Western
Hollywood	

List of Props and Details to Add to Your Theme

Banners	Jukeboxes
Cutouts	Lamps
Entertainers	Mannequins
Feather fans	Masks
Figures – small and life-sized	Neon signs
	Painted backdrops
Games	Photo Boards
Imitation trees	Theme Music

I invite you to my website, *www.partycharlie.com*, where you can shop online for fabulous party items delivered right to your home or office for your perfect party.

Chapter 11

Layout – Making Space for the Party

Making Space

*H*ere are some space-saving techniques that you can plan for days or even weeks in advance:

👪 You may need to move some of your furniture around to accommodate the party. Your home is set up for you to live in on a daily basis — not to throw a party. For instance, your chairs and sofa are most likely focused toward the television. Spread them around the room to encourage guests to mingle.

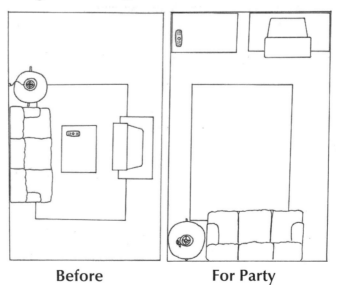

Before   **For Party**

Party Planning Secrets

🏃 Consider moving your furniture to the garage or a spare room and bringing in rental tables and chairs to better accommodate guests.

🏃 Keep in mind that in addition to the space for the tables and chairs, you'll need space for the guests. For instance, a standard-sized dining room table is 8 feet by 4 feet, or 32 square feet, but you'll need space around it for people to walk. For space guidelines, see Chapter 12, "Capacity – How Many Guests Can You Comfortably Accommodate?"

🏃 Use the garage or an extra room in the house as a staging area. Set up one or two tables and use them for storage or to store back-up food and beverages.

🏃 If the kids are away on the night of the party, use their bedroom or a spare room for coats and purses. See Chapter 34, "Coat Check – Planning and Setting Up," for more information and helpful hints.

🏃 Pack away breakable items that are taking up space.

🏃 Turn your kitchen into the buffet area. Clear your counters of anything not being used for the party. Guests always end up congregating in the kitchen, so make the most of every square inch. For example, if you have an island counter in your kitchen and it has chairs around it, remove the chairs.

In order to make the best use of small buffet spaces, build upward. Your display can be on risers, which can be made easily by sliding a box under the tablecloth. For more information, see Chapter 27, "Buffets – How to Design and Set Them Up Effectively."

If you have space in your home, place food stations in various areas. Just make sure none of your guests have to reach over anyone else to get to the food or beverages.

Don't cause a bottleneck at the bar by placing it too close to the buffet, entrance, exit, or restroom, unless the bar is permanent and you don't have a choice. The best place to put the bar is at the far end of your party space. This will encourage guests to enter farther into the party. Don't worry — they'll find it!

Caution: Don't place the bar or buffet station close to the patio or deck edge.

Chapter 12

Capacity — How Many Guests Can You Comfortably Accommodate?

Overall Space Requirements

*B*efore planning your party, make sure you'll have enough space. Here are a few general guidelines to get you started. NOTE: this does not include walking and mingling space. Always consult with your rental companies and vendors for specific space requirements.

Type of Party	Space Requirements
Cocktail party with no seating (using 30-inch stand-up tables)	6–8 sq. ft. per person
Cocktail party with 20%–30% seating (using 30-inch stand-up tables)	10–12 sq. ft. per person
Dinner (using banquet or round tables)	10–12 sq. ft. per person.
Buffet area	100 sq. ft. per table
Bar area	100-150 sq. ft.
Bar area (with 4-ft. back bar)	240 sq. ft. per table
Dance area	3–5 sq. ft. per person
Grand piano	100 sq. ft.
Upright piano	30 sq. ft.
Band or DJ	Consult with provider
Large party props	Consult with provider

Now that you've got some guidelines, just add up what applies to your party. For example, if you're having a dinner party using banquet tables for 100 guests and you have a grand piano, you'll need 1100 square feet (10 sq. ft. per person x 100 guests = 1000 sq. ft. plus 100 sq. ft. for the piano). Of course, you'll want to add space for any bars or buffet stations you might have.

Seating Capacities and Stand-Up Cocktail Tables

The number of people you can seat will depend on the size and type of table. Here are some guidelines:

Size and Type of Table	Seating Capacity
4-ft. (30 x 48 inch) rectangle	4 people
6-ft. (30 x 72 inch) rectangle	6 people
8-ft. (30 x 96 inch) rectangle	8–10 people
36-inch (diameter) round	2–4 people
48-inch round	6–8 people
60-inch round	8–10 people
72-inch round	10–12 people

 You can also rent stand-up cocktail tables, which help the flow of the party and keep the energy going. If you're having a cocktail party, arrange these types of tables throughout the venue.

 30- or 36-inch cocktail tables are great for poolside gatherings or wherever space is an issue.

Stand-up cocktail tables come in various styles, including clear, neon, lacquered, and steel-topped. Ask your rental provider for information about their selections.

A word of advice: use **fewer** of these types of tables than you would need to accommodate all your guests, especially if you're also renting stools for the cocktail tables. That way, people will keep circulating throughout the party area.

Size of Round Cocktail Table	Standing Capacity
30 inch (diameter)	4–6 people
36 inch (diameter)	6–8 people

How Many Seats to Plan For

For a sit-down dinner, seat 100% of your guests.

For a buffet, seat 100% of your guests if there will be presentations, awards, or any type of show.

A true cocktail party has no seats at all. The intention is for people to be up and mingling. But since you do want to accommodate your guests, and we all like to sit and relax after a long day, plan on seating for 20%–30%.

In most venues, such as banquet halls, capacity signs are posted to indicate the maximum number of people. The capacity differs according to whether you're having a stand-up cocktail party or a sit-down dinner.

🎎 There are safety codes for private residences, and you should be aware of them or at least keep to the square footage rules outlined above. Call your local fire department to get specific guidelines for your home. The police department will seldom be summoned to your home unless your music is too loud and you have a history of having parties that get out of control (in which case, you're probably not reading this book).

The Dance Floor

🎎 I recommend estimating three square feet per person.

🎎 Depending on your crowd, 25% to 50% of your guests will be on the dance floor at any given time. So, as you'll read in this book over and over again: know your crowd. This will help you figure out how many people you need to accommodate on the dance floor.

🎎 Most rented dance floors come in 3 x 3-foot or 3 x 4-foot sections.

Chapter 13

Invitations — How to Invite Your Guests

*S*tart creating the energy for your event by tempting your guests with the invitation. Get your guests excited! Your invitation must have some high-energy words, terms like *fun-filled, enchanting,* and *casual but exciting.* Make people want to attend. Just a time and a date will not stimulate excitement or energy.

As hard as it may be to believe, invitations are often an afterthought to many party planners. But the importance of the invitations cannot be overemphasized: It is the first and foremost vehicle used to communicate the appropriate message to your guests! Remember that you get only one chance to make a first impression — make sure it's the right one.

Types of Invitations

Traditional: Traditional-style invitations are printed on various card stocks and envelopes. These can be created professionally, bought ready-made from your local store or created on your own computer.

Internet: Thanks to the Internet, people are able to receive invitations instantly and inexpensively. You can find Internet invitation services like "Evite" *(www.evite.com)* that will allow your guests to see who is coming and how many people to expect. These sites also allow the host to easily set up web pages on which they can post photographs of the party.

E-mail, phone, and word of mouth: For a casual, impromptu invitation, feel free to call, send an e-mail, or encourage invitations by word of mouth.

"Save the Date" Notices

Send a "save the date" teaser about two or three months before your party. The teaser can read something like, "Join us for an incredible, fun-filled party to celebrate [your occasion]. Check your calendar and set aside the date of [month, day, year]. Your official invitation will be coming soon." You want people to come to your party, so the better the teaser, the better the response. Put some creativity into it!

For weddings, a save-the-date notice should be sent four to five months ahead.

When to Send the Invitations

For most parties, send the official invitation at least three weeks before the event.

For a wedding, send the invitation approximately two months before the event. If you didn't send out a "save the date" teaser, make sure the invitations go out at least two months before the event.

Designing the Invitations

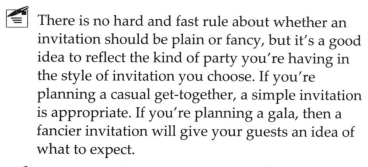 There is no hard and fast rule about whether an invitation should be plain or fancy, but it's a good idea to reflect the kind of party you're having in the style of invitation you choose. If you're planning a casual get-together, a simple invitation is appropriate. If you're planning a gala, then a fancier invitation will give your guests an idea of what to expect.

For printed invitations, keep in mind that printers get very busy, so contact the printer you have selected ASAP and get them printed. That way you'll have plenty of time to check them for errors. Always ask to see a proof! They aren't automatically provided.

The more details, the more time you'll need to design and proof the invitation. Typically wedding, anniversary, bar or bat mitzvah, and other special event invitations require at least two months lead time from your first meeting with the printer to the finished product. For most other invitation styles, about three weeks should be sufficient.

One printer may carry the same type of invitation as another but might charge more for special script styles. Shop around.

Consider making your own invitations to save money. There are many computer programs that help you to create invitations and cards. Predesigned invitations can be found in party, office supply, and stationery stores. You can also add fun and creative details or have your kids decorate the invitations.

What to Include in the Invitations

 No matter what style of invitation you choose, make sure you include high-energy words to get your guests excited and, of course, complete information:

Name:

Type of event: (such as formal wedding, cocktails, dinner, casual BBQ, etc.)

Day and Date: (for example, "Wednesday, June 15th")

Time:

Location/Map:

Attire:

RSVP: (including phone number, e-mail address, and date by which to respond)

 The date and location are important, but so is whether it's indoors or outdoors, casual or formal. This way, your guests can dress comfortably and appropriately.

 Daylight Saving Time may cause some of your guests to arrive either an hour late or an hour early. So if you're hosting a party on the evening of a change in time, include a reminder in your invitation.

 For formal invitations, write the full date and time of the party. Example: *"Saturday, June Tenth, Two Thousand and Six at half past two o'clock in the afternoon."*

For less formal invitations, you don't have to write out the time, and you can leave out the year. Example: "Saturday, June 10, at 2:30 PM."

If you're having a theme party and want the guests to dress in costume, indicate this on your invitations. You'd be amazed how many hosts forget to do this and then end up calling all the invitees to tell them "just one more thing" about the party.

Include directions on your invitations. If you're having a housewarming or a gathering at a venue where most of your guests have never been, go one step further and provide a map. It doesn't have to be elaborate — just a simple drawing will do as long as it's accurate. Cross streets are very helpful.

Let your guests know about special circumstances such as difficult parking or construction in your area.

If you're having a catered party or event with a choice of entrée, provide a menu choice, which can be included on your RSVP card or instructions.

How to Instruct Guests Regarding Attire

The most common question people have after reading an invitation is, "How should I dress?" On your invitation, indicate whether it's casual attire, dressy, black tie, etc. Here are some creative phrases you can use to convey the message:

Casual Attire

Join us for a casual poolside BBQ
Shorts & Tee's
Jacket and ties are banned from this event

Dressy Attire

Dress to impress
Show us your best
Look like a star
Stylish Attire Appreciated

Semiformal

Black Tie optional
Jacket and Tie Welcome

Formal

Black Tie Event
Tuxedo required

Theme

Come in a [fill in the blank] costume
Dress as your favorite [fill in the blank]

Envelopes, Cards, RSVPs, and Thank-You Cards

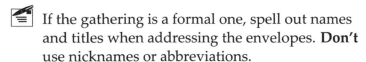 If the gathering is a formal one, spell out names and titles when addressing the envelopes. **Don't** use nicknames or abbreviations.

RSVP stands for *répondez s'il vous plait* (English translation: "Please respond"). Response cards provide a simple way for your guests to let you know if they will attend. Include a stamped envelope printed with the name and address of the person to whom the replies should be sent.

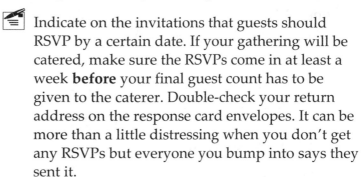 Indicate on the invitations that guests should RSVP by a certain date. If your gathering will be catered, make sure the RSVPs come in at least a week **before** your final guest count has to be given to the caterer. Double-check your return address on the response card envelopes. It can be more than a little distressing when you don't get any RSVPs but everyone you bump into says they sent it.

Guests can also respond to the RSVP for an informal party or event by sending an e-mail RSVP. You can create a separate e-mail account for the event and customize it.

I don't recommend housing out-of-town guests unless they are close family or are unable to drive home. If you're having a gathering where there will be a lot of out-of-town guests, such as a wedding or family reunion, include an accommodation card listing the names and phone numbers of hotels or motels in the area. Include accommodation cards only for out-of-town guests.

If you're hosting a birthday, anniversary, wedding, or any other event where gifts will be given, I think it's necessary to send thank-you cards. (See more about thank you's in Chapter 42, "Thank-You Cards,") If you're having invitations printed, sometimes thank-you cards can be purchased inexpensively if you order them at the same time you order the invitations. In addition, if you're hosting a business party, it's always nice to send cards to thank your guests for attending — especially your VIP clients. It can be a particularly nice gesture to send thank-you cards to any volunteers who might have helped you put the party together.

The Final Word on Invitations

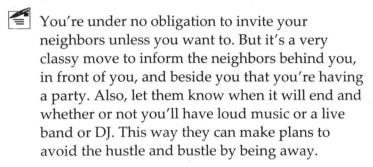 You're under no obligation to invite your neighbors unless you want to. But it's a very classy move to inform the neighbors behind you, in front of you, and beside you that you're having a party. Also, let them know when it will end and whether or not you'll have loud music or a live band or DJ. This way they can make plans to avoid the hustle and bustle by being away.

If you have a neighbor you want to inform about the party but don't want him or her to attend, there are ways of politely getting that across. For example, "We just wanted to alert you that we're hosting a private family party next Saturday and that there will be some music coming from our place. We'll be ending around midnight."

If you want to invite your neighbors, I recommend that you personally deliver the invitation. This is a good way to rekindle or strengthen a relationship.

Save all your responses because you'll want to know who attended when you send thank-you cards.

 It's a good idea to provide a guest book and ask your guests to sign in. Make sure you have a nice-looking pen and a backup pen!

Chapter 14

Menu — What to Serve and When to Serve It

S tep 5 in my Five Steps to 'Create the Energy' for an Outrageously Exciting Party is "Serve Your Guests Fun and Fabulous Food and Beverages." Your menu is important and can sometimes pose a real challenge. I like to say "challenge," but you might call it "a pain in the butt." Or, you may say, "Hey! This is the part I like to do." Either way, here are some tips on menu planning. Again, know your crowd — I can't stress this enough. Of course, sometimes you don't know all the guests who will be attending, so gather some facts, such as the age group.

What to Serve – Know Your Crowd

Think about what your guests like to eat, and serve more of those foods. For instance, for some groups the shrimp appetizers may go like hotcakes. Yet, for specific religious and ethnic groups that don't eat shellfish, you'd have a hard time unloading the shrimp.

Don't repeat a main ingredient. For example, don't serve a shrimp appetizer and a shrimp main dish.

Variety counts. The longer your party and the larger your guest list, the more selections of hors d'oeuvres you should offer.

Balance your selection of hors d'oeuvres. Choose a variety of meat, vegetarian, seafood, cheese, etc.

Hot and cold. Offer both hot and cold foods on a buffet.

Be colorful. Choose a variety of different colors of foods.

Mix your textures. This is particularly true with your side dishes. It's always a good idea to offer something with a crisp topping along with something soft. For example, serve sautéed fresh spinach with onion, fennel, and garlic as well as potatoes au gratin with a crisp, brown, cheesy top.

Choose fun desserts. Dessert makers can provide you with something as simple as white chocolate chip cookies or as extravagant as chocolate desserts in the shape of pianos, race cars, or movie film. You can have desserts with photo-quality images printed on sugar paper. You can even rent chocolate fountains circulating melted chocolate for dipping fresh fruits and an assortment of treats! However, chocolate fountains make a chocolate mess! Don't use fine linen under them.

Review the food topics in this book. For more information on food transport, preparation, and quantities, see Chapter 17, "Food – Preparing

Your Own" and Chapter 16, "Food – How to Transport It from the Market or Restaurant to Home."

When to Serve It – How to Make a Timetable for Your Party

It's a good idea to have a basic schedule of how you want your party to flow. If you don't have a schedule, the cocktail "hour" may turn into three hours, and your guests will get tanked before it's time to eat. Here are some guidelines you can use.

Cocktail party before dinner: 1 hour. When considering the amount of hors d'oeuvres per person, keep in mind that you want your guests to enjoy the dinner. Some people want a decadent cocktail party because they feel that starts the event rolling. If you can afford it, go for it! Keep in mind that smaller portions in the main course are highly recommended.

Cocktail party only: 1–3 hours. If you're not serving dinner, make sure the hors d'oeuvres are hearty. Items with bread, puff pastry, or mini rolls work well. An example is thinly sliced tenderloin of beef served on a mini brioche roll topped with black pepper sour cream horseradish. You should start serving the hors d'oeuvres at the time the invitation states. Having a stationary hors d'oeuvres buffet is a great idea so guests can help themselves. Remember to provide a variety of selections, such as beef, chicken, seafood, cheeses, and vegetarian items on your menu.

Cocktail party with dessert: 1–3 hours. Yes, you can have a cocktail party and serve dessert. If your party is going to be less than 1½ hours, I recommend that you set out the dessert at the beginning of the reception along with the hors d'oeuvres.

Basic dinner party: 4 hours. Dinner parties can be a fun way of entertaining. Any occasion can be celebrated with a basic dinner party.

> *Time line for basic dinner party:*
> 1 hour – cocktails and mingling
> 1½ half hours – dinner and toast
> 1 hour – ceremonial cake-cutting or dessert
> 30 minutes – wind-down time

Business luncheon: 2 hours maximum. People are busy and will need to get to work. Whether you're providing a buffet or a sit-down meal, be sure to offer a choice of foods for your guests — a one-item entrée will not work. Feed your guests before you attempt to make any speeches. Trust me: when the natives are restless, their attention drops! It's alright to serve while the speeches are going on. Usually it is best to stop serving before the keynote speaker is introduced.

> *Time line for business luncheon:*
> 15 minutes – guests mingle
> 1 hour – soup, salad, main course,
>   or buffet service
> 30 minutes – dessert and coffee
> 15 minutes – wind down

Party Planning Secrets

Event luncheon: 3–4 hours. Most luncheons include a three-course meal or a buffet with several choices. A sit-down luncheon consists of salad or soup and then the main dish, followed by dessert and coffee. Festivities, honors, awards, and so on take place during lunch and dessert.

Time line for event luncheon:
15 minutes – guests mingle
15 minutes – quick introduction
1½ hours – soup, salad, main course,
   or buffet service
1 hour – dessert and coffee
30 minutes – wind-down announcements

Party luncheon: 3–4 hours. Same as the event luncheon, except there may be dancing. If you will offer dancing, your music should be playing 40 minutes on and 20 minutes off in order to get guests back to their seats for toasts, speeches, etc. This should be timed to the service of the food.

Wedding: 5 hours not including the ceremony. Dancing is going on throughout the celebration.

Time line for wedding:
1 hour – cocktail party
1 hour – grand entrance, first dance,
   guests join in
1 hour – dinner, toast
1 hour – throwing of the bouquet and garter
1 hour – dessert and goodbyes

There can be several toasts throughout the wedding. Traditionally, the best man gives the

toast before or during the meal or before the cake cutting. This is by no means the only way to schedule your wedding celebration. You can have a first dance and toast before the cake cutting. Yes I'm aware of proper protocol; however, it's your day, so, do what makes you feel comfortable!

Child's birthday party: 2½–3 hours. Keep the children entertained! Have food and beverages available from start to finish. Children seem to have their own time schedule. How do I know? I used to be one!

> *Time line for child's birthday party:*
> Snacks and beverages available all the time
> 30 minutes – mingling and strolling
>   entertainment
> 30 minutes – games
> 30 minutes – main meal (or just set out
>   a wonderful selection of snacks)
> 30 minutes – entertainment (such as a
>   magic or puppet show)
> 15 minutes – cake cutting
> 15 minutes – opening presents
> 15 minutes – final game, entertainment,
>   or presentation (such as a balloon artist)
>   to provide a gift for each child to take home

Brunch: 2–4 hours. Brunches are a favorite of mine because they combine breakfast and lunch items. You must have all the food ready to serve when the guests arrive for a brunch. The water and juices must be available and coffee ready, and if you're serving champagne or mimosas (equal parts champagne and orange juice), make sure they're chilled and ready to go. Put the champagne on ice and the OJ in a pitcher.

Time line for brunch :
This depends on your occasion. You can celebrate any type of event with a brunch. Then apply the rules above to plan your time line.

Toasting Tips

There are many ways to give a toast. When we hear a toast, we usually think of a wedding, where the best man gives a short, eloquent, and wonderful speech. Or perhaps it was short, funny, and cute. A brief, cleverly crafted speech is the number one key to a successful toast.

A toast should start with a welcome to your guests on behalf of you and your significant other, or whoever has a part in hosting the event. Acknowledge the important people, whether they are the elders, your immediate family, or business colleagues. Here are some guidelines for your toast:

1. **It should be warm.**
2. **It should be funny.**
3. **It should be cute.**
4. **It should include your guests.**
5. **Most of all, it should be short!**

For the wedding or anniversary toast by the host, include a brief, cute story how you and your wife met. For the best man's toast, talk about how you and the groom met, or a cute story about the bride and groom. *Never mention past love relationships of the bride or groom.* In a business toast, welcome the guest on behalf of the company.

The toast can work as a great icebreaker to welcome everyone and reiterate the purpose of the gathering.

Chapter 15

Food – Make Room for It

The Refrigerator – Using It Wisely

*Y*our refrigerator is your best ally when having an event in your home. Make sure it's clean, empty, and ready to accommodate your party food supplies.

I'm not sure why folks don't like to part with their three-year-old mustard, but the response I hear most often when I'm helping someone clear out their refrigerator for a party is, "Oh, we still use that." When there are items in your fridge that are old enough to have voted for our last president, it's time to toss them out.

Making the Most of Your Refrigerator Space

When you're throwing a party, space in your refrigerator is at a premium. Here are some tips for maximizing space for items that have to be kept cold.

- Buy or borrow an ice chest or two, depending on the size of the party.

- Take an inventory of what's inside your refrigerator. Combine duplicate items as long as the dates don't differ.

- Remove items that are past their prime. You can even make a game out of getting rid of food past the expiration date by having your kids do it.

Whoever comes up with the greatest amount of old food wins a prize.

There's no need to store beverages in your refrigerator for your party. Most require only an hour and a half in an ice chest topped off with ice to completely chill.

Use zipper-top-style bags to store your food. They will easily conform to the area of the refrigerator. You can also use stackable plastic containers. Have several sizes available; be sure to use the size that best fits the food item you're storing. Sometimes you might fill a plastic container only halfway — the other half is wasted space.

If your freezer has built up a two-inch layer of ice, it's time to defrost. Get this done as soon as you can.

Now That Your Refrigerator and Freezer Are Cleaned Out...

Put meat, chicken, and seafood for the party on the bottom shelf of the fridge. Put them in a pan in addition to the wrapper in which they came. Once food products start to thaw, some of the juices may spill out. Use a pan with a lip to catch the liquid.

The items you'll need first for your food preparation should be placed in the front of the fridge.

It's best to reserve freezer space for frozen foods rather than ice. Ice is cheap — buy it. For tips on

buying ice, such as how much you'll need, check out Chapter 49, "Keeping Your Party Cool."

Check the temperature of your refrigerator and freezer. In order to prevent microorganisms from growing, run the refrigerator at a maximum of 40 degrees Fahrenheit. The freezer temperature should be set at 0 degrees Fahrenheit or lower. You can check the temperature of your refrigerator and freezer with a simple appliance thermometer.

Chapter 16

Food — How To Transport It from the Market or Restaurant to Home

*O*rdering food from your favorite restaurant is a great time saver. Here's how to make it work for you.

How to Get Your Food Home

🍽 Ask the catering service at the market or restaurant to "cater-wrap" the order. What is cater-wrapping? Well, it's a PartyCharlie-ism that can best be explained as really tight, clear film wrapping. Cater-wrapping involves pulling the film wrap out onto the surface of the table, placing the item on the film, tightly wrapping the film around the item, and repeating until all surfaces are completely covered. If the market or

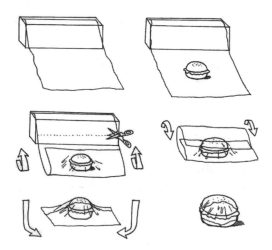

restaurant doesn't know what you mean, just show them the diagram on the previous page.

🍽 Ask the restaurant to place your food in a disposable pan that will fit in your oven. Of course, you'll need to know the interior size of the oven, from side to side and front to back.

🍽 Make the food pickup your last errand so you don't end up leaving the food in the car while you attend to other tasks.

🍽 If you're transporting perishable items and your trip will take more than an hour, put the food in an ice chest or Styrofoam® unit.

🍽 Ice packs work well, or as you will see in Chapter 49, "Keeping Your Party Cool," you can use my thin ice tip for transporting food. Instead of packing foods in loose ice, which melts and gets messy, fill a plastic freezer bag with enough water so that when you seal and lay it on a flat surface, there's about an inch thickness of water. Place it in your freezer. When it's frozen, it will be a sheet of ice. You can make several ice sheets at once and place them on top of one another to freeze.

🍽 Don't put packages of food on top of one another in the car. They can and probably will get crushed.

🍽 Make sure the items are secure in the car so they don't slide off the seat and onto the floor. Storing them on the floor helps. Or you can sometimes even secure them onto the back of the seat using seatbelts.

What To Do Once You Get Your Food Home

🍽 As I mentioned in the section "Refrigerator – Using It Wisely" (Chapter 15), check the temperature of your refrigerator and freezer. If you aren't planning to use the fresh meat, poultry, or fish you've purchased within two days, freeze it immediately.

🍽 If you purchase a product that has a label reading "Keep Refrigerated," guess what? Yup, it **has** to be refrigerated.

🍽 Refrigerate all dairy products promptly.

🍽 Cold foods that tend to spoil easily without refrigeration shouldn't be exposed to warm temperatures for more than 30 minutes before you set them out for your guests to eat.

🍽 Hot foods that were picked up just before the party should be eaten no more than two hours after they leave the store and should be kept at 140 degrees fahrenheit or hotter.

Chapter 17

Food — Preparing Your Own

$\mathcal{I}$f you're preparing food at home, there are some things you should know.

Food Safety

🏴 **Never** leave perishable foods such as meat, poultry, eggs, and casseroles in the sun.

🏴 Wash your hands, including your fingernails, before you begin any type of food preparation. Wash vigorously with hot water for at least 20 seconds. If you have to stop at any time to answer the phone, feed your pet, scratch your nose, or take out the garbage, wash your hands AGAIN.

🏴 Cloth towels retain bacteria, so after washing your hands, dry them with paper towels.

🏴 If you have any cuts on your hands, cover them tightly with a bandage and wear plastic gloves. Cuts breed germs, which can be transferred to the food.

Party Planning Secrets

🎏 Tie your hair behind you, and if you can stand it, wear a hairnet.

🎏 Don't allow anyone to smoke around the food you're preparing.

🎏 After contact with any raw foods, always wash kitchen countertops, dishes, cutting boards, and utensils thoroughly with hot, soapy water, bleach, or a sanitizing solution. You can make your own sanitizing solution by adding 1 tablespoon of unscented bleach to 1 gallon of warm water.

🎏 Be sure to clean up as you go. A mess can pile up quickly. Believe me, it is much easier to wipe a knife and put it back where it belongs than to throw it in the sink with tons of other dishes, pots, pans, etc. This way you avoid cutting yourself when you reach into the sink.

🎏 Clean — don't just rinse — your utensils.

🎏 Use separate cutting boards for raw and cooked foods.

🎏 Always thaw foods in the refrigerator or in cold water. Make sure you change the water every 30 minutes. **Never thaw foods in hot water.** Hot water breeds bacteria.

🎏 Don't refrigerate hot food. Let it cool slightly at room temperature before refrigerating.

🎏 Always marinate meat in the refrigerator. Again, those pesky germs can build up, so place the meat

in zipper-style bags or stacking containers for easy storage.

Refrigerate all dairy products promptly, including foods made from dry mixes, such as sauces, puddings, and dressings.

Make sure all foods are properly dated and labeled.

As I mentioned in "The Refrigerator – Using It Wisely" (Chapter 15), check the temperature of your refrigerator and freezer.

The only safe way to make sure that your food is cooked to the desired temperature is to use a food thermometer. This way, that expensive rib roast will be edible. Food thermometers work well for any meat or poultry.

PartyCharlie's Cooking Guide

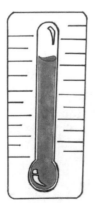

Make sure your meats reach the following temperatures before considering them "done" (refer to pages 94-95). Check temperature in several places to be sure the food is evenly heated. Wash the thermometer with hot, soapy water after use.

Several types of thermometers are available:

Oven-safe thermometers can be inserted at the beginning of the cooking time 2 to 2½ inches into the thickest part of the food. It remains there throughout cooking.

🌡 **Instant-read thermometers** are not designed to stay in the food during cooking. Insert the probe the full length of the sensing area, usually 2 to 2½ inches. If you're measuring the temperature of a roast or turkey, insert the probe sideways with the sensing device in the center of your food. About 15 to 20 seconds will be required for the temperature to be accurately displayed.

🌡 **Digital instant-read thermometers** are not designed to stay in food during cooking. The heat-sensing device is in the tip of the probe. Place the tip of the probe in the center of the thickest part of the food, at least ½ inch deep. After 10 seconds, the temperature will be accurately displayed.

Internal Cooking Temperatures

Product	Temperature (F)
Egg & Egg Dishes	
Eggs	Cook until yolk and white are firm.
Egg casseroles	160 degrees
Egg sauces, custards	160 degrees
Ground Meat & Meat Mixtures	
Turkey, chicken	165 degrees
Beef, veal, lamb, pork	160 degrees
Fresh Beef, Veal, Lamb	
Medium rare	145 degrees
Medium	160 degrees
Well done	170 degrees
Fresh Pork	
Medium	160 degrees
Well done	170 degrees
Ham	
Fresh (raw)	160 degrees
Fully cooked (to reheat)	140 degrees
Roast Beef	
Cooked commercially, vacuum sealed and ready-to-eat	140 degrees
Poultry, Foul	
Chicken, turkey (whole)	180 degrees
Chicken, turkey (dark meat)	180 degrees
Chicken or turkey breast	170 degrees
Duck and goose	180 degrees
Stuffing	
Cooked alone or in bird	165 degrees

Product	Temperature (F)
Sauces, Soups, Gravies, Marinades	
Used with raw meat, poultry, or fish	Bring to a rapid boil.
Seafood	
Fish	Cook until opaque and flakes easily with a fork. Check center of one piece.
Shrimp, lobster, crab	Should turn red and flesh should become pearly white. Check center of one piece
Scallops	Should turn milky white or opaque and firm. If sautéing, check center of one piece.
Clams, mussels, oysters	Cook until shells open. Discard any that don't open.
Leftovers	165 degrees

Note: When cooking for larger groups, it's important to test at least one piece before serving.

Helpful Food Prep Tips

🍽️ If you're throwing a really big party and have little or no experience in the kitchen, I strongly recommend hiring a helper with some food prep knowledge. Even if the helper is only going to chop vegetables and tidy up for you, it will be helpful to have someone with a little cooking experience.

🍽 Trim the fats off meats in advance.

🍽 Some foods can be cut a day in advance of the party, which will save you lots of time. Basically, cut anything that won't spoil or turn color. This includes most vegetables, thicker-skinned fruits, and many meats.

🍽 Avoid cutting thin-skinned fruits in advance because they oxidize. For instance, apples, pears, peaches, and plums turn brown if you cut them too early. In fact, you don't have to cut them at all — you can do a nice display of whole and cut fruits. Cut the ones that don't oxidize, such as melons and strawberries. Leave whole fruits such as apples, pears, plums, and peaches for a whole-fruit display in a basket.

🍽 Keep each type of cut fruit in separate bags. This way you can put them out in a display just before your guests arrive.

🍽 Certain fruits, especially berries, have dark juices that will mix with the other juices and will overpower the flavor of other fruits.

🍽 Make marinades, dressings, and dips a day or two in advance.

🍽 Never try new recipes on the day of your party. Make the dish a week or so in advance as a practice run.

Many Uses for Styrofoam® Units

Styrofoam® units are widely available in supermarkets and other stores.

🍽 People usually think of the Styrofoam® ice chest for cold foods and drinks but not for hot food. Styro units are thermo units. They keep cold food cold and temporarily keep hot food hot.

🍽 Use small styros for side dishes and larger ones for entrées. You can also use them for transporting foods and as storage while you're making the rest of your meal.

🍽 Whether you're hosting a dinner, a large party, or a backyard barbeque, use large styros to reduce overcrowding in your fridge or oven. You can also lend or give small styros to guests who are bringing food or taking it home with them.

🍽 Theme decorations or colorful wrapping paper can be placed around the units to make them festive no matter what the occasion.

Keep Hot Foods Hot

We all know that ice chests can keep food cold, but here's something that most people have never thought of before. You can also use your ice chest to temporarily keep hot foods hot, for 30 minutes or so. Like a Styrofoam® unit, an ice chest is really just a thermal unit, so regardless of whether it's holding in the cold or heat, its job is to maintain the temperature. Follow these steps to turn your ice chest into a warmer:

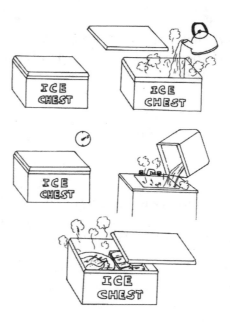

1. Pour 1 gallon of boiling water into the ice chest. If your tap water gets really hot, fill the chest with 1 gallon of hot tap water.

2. Close the lid and let it sit for about 5 minutes. That's just enough to warm up the interior of the chest.

3. Carefully empty out the water.

4. Wrap up your food items and place them into the warm chest.

    Caution: Do not use the warmed ice chest to keep food warm for the duration of a party. Use this technique only for keeping food warm just before serving it.

Food Quantities

The key to food quantities is to **know your guests.** For instance, a group of women at a luncheon tend to eat a lot less than a high school basketball team gathering to celebrate another win. People will eat less at a memorial service than they will at a holiday party.

- When I cater a party for my clients, running out of something is not an option. When you're catering your own party and you run out of something, it's not the end of the world.

- The more choices you offer on your menu, the smaller your calculation of individual portion size has to be. (See the next page for tips on portion sizes.)

- Use "filler" food. For cocktail parties, provide plenty of snack foods like pretzels and nuts in addition to any appetizers you're serving.

- People will eat much more savory side dishes like broccoli casserole and whipped potatoes with mushrooms than they will sweet side dishes like glazed carrots.

- People tend to eat more starches and meats than they do vegetables.

- Fried foods are always the first to go at a party.

- Sheet cakes come in standard sizes such as a quarter sheet, half sheet, and full sheet. A full sheet serves 100 people on average. Depending on the size of your crowd, a quarter sheet could very well serve your whole party. Not everyone eats cake, and you can always cut smaller pieces.

🍽 When you offer multiple desserts, people will taste small portions of more items. On average, 10% of your guests will not have dessert when you're serving a buffet-style meal. Order the "mini" version of multiple desserts so your guests can sample.

🍽 To help you prepare for any occasion, I have provided a range by which you can plan how much food to serve per portion. Multiply your estimates by the number of guests and then round up the amount.

PartyCharlie Portion Sizes

Individual meats, fish, poultry	5-6 ounces per person
Multiple meat meals and buffets	4–5 ounces per person
Pasta – for a sit-down dinner	1 pound of pasta will serve 4–6
Pasta – for a buffet with other foods	1 pound of pasta will serve 8–10
Premixed salad	One handful per person (1 ½ ounce)
Hors d'oeuvres – when serving dinner	3–6 per person
Hors d'oeuvres – when not serving dinner	5–10 per person
Side dishes – savory	2 side dishes per person at ½ cup each
Side dishes – sweet	1 side dish per person at ½ cup each
Dessert – with dinner	1 full portion per person
Dessert only	1½ portions per person

Chapter 18

Potluck – Organizing a Successful Event

Twelve Steps to Potluck Success

1. Decide how many people will be at your potluck. Take into consideration that you'll be asking guests to make their favorite or appropriate food or beverage item. Remember, a couple living together will most likely bring one prepared item.

2. You can send invitations for a potluck, but make sure you indicate that it's a potluck and that if guests want to participate, they need to RSVP two weeks in advance or ASAP in order to confirm what they're bringing.

3. Decide what you want to make. In general, the host provides the main dish and the guests provide the appetizers, side dishes, desserts, and beverages. Make a list of food and beverage items that you'd like guests to provide. Some people may want to prepare a special recipe, and if so, let them. But for those who don't know what they want to bring, be prepared to present some suggestions from your list.

4. Let guests know how much food or beverage they should bring. Use tips in the "PartyCharlie Portion Sizes" section from Chapter 17, "Food – Preparing Your Own," as well as the beverage amounts from Chapter 29, "Bars – Full Service."

5. If your guests are transporting the food in aluminum tins, casserole dishes, etc., tell them how to "cater-wrap" their food items (you'll find this tip in Chapter 16, "Food – How to Transport It from the Market or Restaurant to Home").

6. If your guests are transporting food in something other than the serving dish, such as an aluminum tin, ask them if they can bring along a serving dish as well. Just remember to tell them not to bring anything irreplaceable, in case the piece should become damaged.

7. If guests need to cook or heat up their dishes at the party location, ask them the size and dimensions of the casserole dish or pan so you can make sure their cookware can fit in your oven. Measure your oven's interior cooking space. It's a good idea to limit the number of guests needing to use the oven. Keep it fun and simple.

    Tip: Preheat your oven before guests arrive so it's warm in case they need to keep their dish warm.

8. Ask guests the size of the serving platter, dish, or basket they're putting their food or beverage in. You'll need the dimensions to figure out your food and beverage placement for your buffet table.

9. Once you have a handle on what everyone is bringing, plan the buffet using **The PartyCharlie 1-2-3 Step.** You can find instructions in Chapter 28, "Buffet Organization."

10. Create cards with the name of the dish and the person who brought it.

11. Two days before the party, confirm each menu item with the guest preparing it.

12. **Make sure you thank each guest individually for his or her contribution.** When a guest comes in with the dish, don't say, "Oh, just put it over there." Thank him or her for taking the time and effort to prepare the food.

Chapter 19

BBQ — Keeping It Safe, Clean, and Hot

$\mathcal{B}$arbeque parties are fun, especially because you get to enjoy the outdoors, and they're generally casual.

You can turn the BBQ party into a potluck by asking your friends to bring their main course — chicken, beef, or fish. Then get them involved by having them cook their own entrée. Be sure to tell them how to keep the raw food safe during transport (see Chapter 16 for tips on transporting food safely). Provide an ice chest or make room in the refrigerator for the food your guests are bringing.

You can provide the appetizers, salads, side dishes, and desserts. Set up the buffet and self-service bar, and let the party begin!

Keeping It Safe, Clean, and Hot

The basic ways to make your barbeque a success are to keep the fire going, keep the grill clean, keep the bugs away (see Chapter 20), keep the grilling area safe, and keep it well lit. Below are some tips on accomplishing these tasks.

Here is a list of tools I recommend you have on hand:

- Long-handled tongs and spatulas for turning grilled foods and handling the coals

- Spray bottle filled with water

- Disposable aluminum tray for heating side foods like baked beans

- BBQ shovel and long-handled spoon

- Wire grill brush for cleaning the grill

- Insulated, flame-retardant gloves

Keep the Coal Fire Burning

- Remove the grill. Place your charcoal in the belly of the barbecue and stack it in a pyramid shape.

- Use starter coals. They're fast and easy to use because they're already infused with lighter fluid.

- If your grill doesn't have a holding or warming level, reserve a section of the grill where there is little or no coal at all. This will be your holding area for food that's done but needs to be kept warm.

- Let all the lighter fluid burn away before you start cooking.

- When coals turn gray, level them out with a long-handled spoon or BBQ shovel. Remember to reserve space for the warming section.

🌡 Use the spray bottle to spritz flare-ups, which can blacken your food.

Fire Warning

Do not spray lighter fluid on the fire to create a spectacular fireball. The fire will go out in a few seconds because most of the lighter fluid vaporizes before it reaches the charcoal. But before it goes out, it may very well singe off your eyebrows.

The Grilling Surface

🌡 To ensure that food won't stick to the grilling surface, spray or brush it with vegetable oil before lighting. Do **not** spray vegetable oil on the grill while coals are burning.

🌡 Make sure that the grilling surface is **HOT** before putting any food on it. You can check with one piece of food by placing it on the grill. If it sizzles, it's ready.

Cleaning the Grill

Always check the manufacturer's instructions about cleaning, but if you misplace them or threw them away, here are some helpful tips.

🌡 Sprinkle baking soda on a damp brush. Scrub the grill and rinse it clean.

🌡 Place your grill rack in an inconspicuous area on the grass or patio and spray it with household cleaner. Let it sit overnight. The dew will work with the cleaner so that by morning, you can just hose off the grill. But be aware that this can damage your grass. Do not use this method in an area where children and pets play.

🌡 Use a steel grill brush to clean off the major food. Then pop the grill rack into your self-cleaning oven. This will clean your grill and your oven at the same time.

Keeping the Barbeque Safe – Do's and Don'ts

See Chapter 7, "Safety – Making It a Priority" for more safety tips.

Do's:

- **Do** keep a bucket of water or a garden hose nearby in case of accidents. A bucket of sand is also good to keep around.

- **Do** keep the barbeque area well lit. This is not only important for ensuring accurate cooking, but it will help prevent any accidents that might occur while you're grilling in the dark.

- **Do** keep your grill on level ground.

- **Do** set up the grill on a nonflammable surface such as brick, concrete, or dirt.

- **Do** keep your grill away from buildings, trees, and shrubs.

- **Do** keep your grill away from windy areas.

- **Do** keep kids and pets away from the grill.

- **Do** check the gas line and hoses for leaks before using them, especially after they've been in storage for the winter. Do this by dabbing the joints with soapy water before use. If you see bubbles, you may have a leak.

- **Do** take your phone to the grill with you, so you don't have to run into the house when it rings.

- **Do** read the instructions before you use any barbeque lighting product. And then, guess what? Do **follow the instructions.**

- **Do** keep a fire extinguisher handy.

Don'ts:

🌡 **Don't** grill inside a tent or other enclosed area.

🌡 **Don't** use gasoline or other flammable liquids not designed for a barbeque.

🌡 **Don't** leave a grill unattended once it is lit.

🌡 **Don't** move a lit barbeque. It can easily tip over.

🌡 **Don't** drink alcohol while you're grilling. You need to be able to stay focused and clear-headed.

🌡 **Don't** set the grill on or near wood or simulated wood materials or next to your house.

Using a Fire Extinguisher

Follow the fire department's "PASS system":

1. Pull the pin.

2. Aim the extinguisher nozzle at the **base** of the flames.

3. Squeeze the trigger while holding the extinguisher upright.

4. Sweep the extinguisher from side to side, covering the area of the fire with the extinguishing agent.

Chapter 20

Insects — The Uninvited Guests

🕷 Well before your guests arrive, spray the rims of your trash cans with insecticide to keep away bees and crawling bugs. Doing this well in advance will ensure that your guests won't smell the insecticide.

🕷 Set up citronella candles around the party perimeters to keep mosquitoes away. Make sure the candles are safe, level, and in open, well-ventilated areas.

🕷 Put the legs of your tables into four sturdy pans or bowls of water. Ants won't be able to cross the water and thus won't be able to climb up the table legs.

🕷 Sprinkle salt around the area where you'll be eating. Ants won't cross over the salt trails that you put in the grass.

🕷 Wash the top of your table with white vinegar. Most insects hate vinegar.

Section 3

PRESENTATION: PUTTING IT ALL TOGETHER

Chapter 21

Table Coverings — Linens and Paper

Table Covering Options

🍽 When purchasing fabric from your local fabric store, pick out a wonderful print or solid that goes with your theme.

🍽 Paper table coverings are an inexpensive way to decorate your tables without having to rent table linens. Paper coverings come in a wide variety of colors, patterns, and themes.

🍽 If you do want table linens, companies that rent tables and chairs also generally rent a wide variety of linens. You can find anything from traditional damask to contemporary patterns to stripes, plaids, themed, and checked patterns.

🍽 After the party, **do not** place your linens in plastic bags. They can get thrown out; and even if they don't get thrown out, mold can develop. And mold doesn't come out, so if you rented the linens, you'll be charged for the replacement cost. Keep them dry until you drop them off or they are picked up. Dry soiled linens can be rolled into a ball.

What You'll Need for Round Tables

The following diagrams will help you figure out the table covering size you'll need for your round tables so your linen drapes to the ground. You can also ask the rental company to recommend a linen size for any odd-sized tables that you may own.

Table Size	30"	36"
Linen Size	90 inches round	90 inches round
Table Size	42"	48"
Linen Size	102 inches round	108 inches round
Table Size	54"	60"
Linen Size	108 inches round	120 inches round
Table Size	66"	72"
Linen Size	120 inches round	132 inches round

If your event is casual, you can cover the table with a cloth that is long enough to drape over the table edge. It doesn't have to reach the floor.

What You'll Need for Banquet Tables

The following diagrams will help you figure out the size of table coverings you'll need for your banquet tables.

Banquet Tables

Table Size	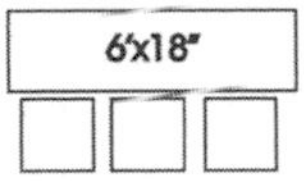 6'x18"	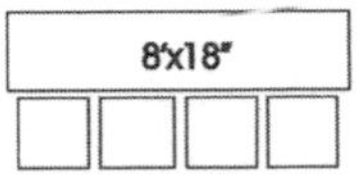 8'x18"
Linen Size	10-foot banquet	10- or 12-foot banquet
Table Size	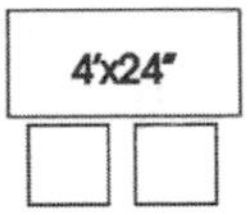 4'x24"	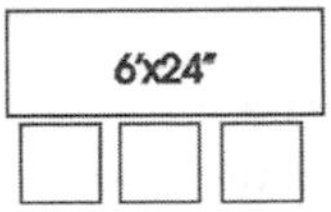 6'x24"
Linen Size	10-foot banquet folded	10-foot banquet
Table Size	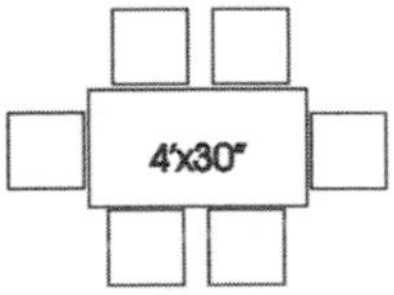 4'x30"	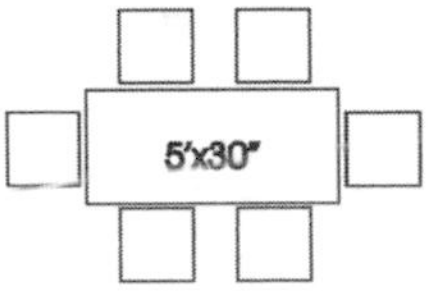 5'x30"
Linen Size	10-foot banquet folded	10-foot banquet
Table Size	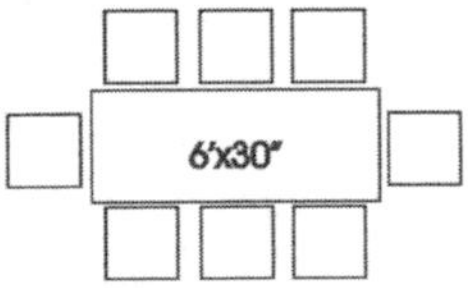 6'x30"	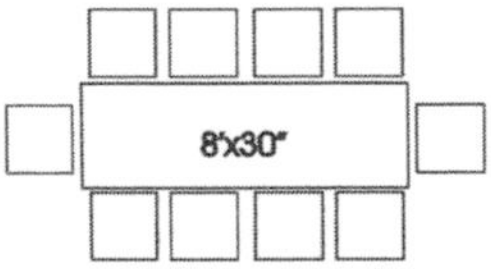 8'x30"
Linen Size	10-foot banquet	10- or 12-foot banquet

Table Size	6'x40"	8'x40"
Linen Size	10-foot banquet	12-foot banquet
Table Size	30"	48"
Linen Size	90 inches	102 or108 inches

Party rental companies are always helpful in recommending your linen options, such as sizes, colors and overlays.

Chapter 22

Table Setting —
What Goes Where

*M*ost of us just grab a fork and start devouring what's on the plate (or at least I do), but there is actually a method to setting a table. I've included a full table-setting diagram below. You don't have to use all these utensils, glasses, and plates if you don't want to.

Below is an example of a formal setting. If you plan to use this type of service, I highly recommend that you read my tips on hiring staff in Chapter 43, "Vendors and Rentals."

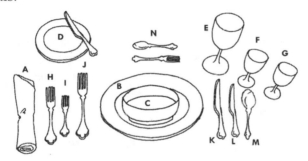

A. Napkin	**H.** Salad fork
B. Service plate	**I.** Fish fork
C. Soup bowl on plate	**J.** Dinner fork
D. Bread plate with butter knife	**K.** Service knife
	L. Fish knife
E. Water glass	**M.** Soup spoon
F. White wine	**N.** Dessert spoon and cake fork
G. Red wine	

When you have staff helping you, set one place at the table to demonstrate how you want the rest of the settings done.

Chapter 23

Disposable Ware – Making It Easy with Napkins, Plates, Utensils, and Drink Ware

PartyCharlie Tips

🍽 As soon as you know you're having a party, watch for sales.

🍽 In party planning, **last minute = more money + more stress.** So shop early for disposable ware. Buying patterned disposable ware early might help avoid a problem if the store runs out of your pattern.

🍽 Buy only heavy-duty ware, whether it's paper or plastic.

Paper Napkins

🍽 Paper napkins come in three standard sizes. Make sure you buy at least the minimum thickness, which is called "2-ply" or, more commonly, "double ply."

> Cocktail 5" x 5" (small)
> Luncheon 12-7/8" x 12-7/8" (medium)
> Dinner 15" x 17" (large)

- Consider the type of food you're serving. For instance, if you're having messy food such as barbeque, you'll want to use dinner napkins regardless of whether it's a dinner or lunch gathering. If you're only offering coffee and dessert (cookies or brownies, for example), then luncheon or cocktail napkins are just fine.

- If you're having a barbeque or serving finger foods, you might want to have disposable hand wipes or wet napkins available.

- Make sure you have **extra** napkins. People will use them for dinner, dessert, and drinks.

Cloth Napkins

You can add a fancy touch to your table setting by using cloth napkins. This is perfectly acceptable even if you're using disposable plates and utensils. To see examples of 12 different ways to fold napkins, go to "Cloth Napkin-Folding Instructions," in the Appendix.

Plates

- Whether you're using designer disposable ware or standard disposables from your local supermarket or party store, make sure they're sturdy enough to withstand a full meal and won't allow food juices or sauces to soak through.

- Provide additional plates. At buffet restaurants, people are used to getting new plates each time they visit the buffet. I recommend two per person.

Don't forget the bowls if you're having soup or salad, side dishes, or ice cream.

If you're having a small sit-down dinner party, feel free to put out the nice china. Don't use anything that would devastate you if it gets broken, such as plates that have been passed down from generation to generation. Even if you're having a small number of guests, it's still a party, and accidents happen.

Line your sink with a soft towel to ensure safety when washing expensive or fragile dishes and glassware by hand.

You can always rent plates for a large party, but don't feel you have to. Some disposable plates look like fine china. Most party stores carry plates with marble and faux wood designs.

Utensils

Make sure you have plenty of forks, knives, and spoons. It's easy to think, for instance, "Oh, I don't need spoons — we're not having dessert." And then when the soup bowls come out, the next thing you'll hear is "Hey, you forgot the spoons!"

If you're using plastic utensils, make sure the knives are strong enough to cut any meat you're serving and that the forks and spoons won't snap off in your food.

Drink Ware

There are many types of plastic drink ware from which to choose. I recommend 10-ounce clear plastic tumblers. However, I recognize that some people like to have different sizes for different beverages (mixed drinks, wine, etc.). And if you're doing a champagne toast, I agree that it's best to have a special glass for it. Below are some types of plastic drink ware that are readily available.

- 4-ounce plastic champagne glasses
- 5-ounce plastic wine glasses
- 12-ounce plastic margarita glasses
- 6-ounce plastic martini glasses
- 10-ounce all-purpose plastic tumblers
- 16-ounce all-purpose plastic tumblers (beer)

Disposable Ware Quantities

Generally speaking, you'll be buying your disposable ware in bulk packaging. Recommended quantities for each guest, based on a five-hour party, are shown below:

3–4 tumblers
2–3 cocktail napkins
2–3 dinner napkins (4–5 if you're serving
　　　messy food such as BBQ or if you're
　　　having a lot of children)
1–2 dinner plates (2 if you're having buffet style)
1 dessert plate
1 bowl per menu item requiring a bowl
3 forks (1 for dinner, 1 for dessert, 1 for
　　　backup)

1 spoon or swizzle stick (you may need
   additional spoons if you're serving soup, etc.)
1 coffee cup

Check out my website, *www.partycharlie.com*, where
you can shop online for fabulous party items delivered
right to your home or office for your perfect party.

Chapter 24

Equipment — If You Don't Have It, Borrow It

$\mathcal{B}$uying equipment for your party is fine if you think you're going to use it over and over. Then you'll get your money's worth. But for those of you who aren't planning on a career in the catering/party planning business, there's no reason you can't borrow the items you need from friends.

The Six Golden Rules For Borrowing

1. Don't borrow anything you can't afford to replace.

2. Don't borrow antiques or other irreplaceable items.

3. Tell the person you're borrowing from up-front that you'll replace the item if it gets damaged. This will let him or her know you're serious about taking care of it.

4. You don't have to watch borrowed items like a hawk, but make sure you use them for their intended purpose, and place them in areas where they will be safe.

5. Always replace damaged items immediately. This is a good way to keep your friendship.

6. Make a list of what you've borrowed from whom so you'll remember when it's time to give the items back to the proper owner.

Some Handy Items to Borrow

Beverage pitchers	Hurricane glass for candles
Blenders	Ice chests
Candle holders	Lights
Chafing dishes	Linens
Chairs	Plants
Chilling tubs	Plates – dinner and dessert
Coffeemakers	Popcorn maker
Cooking utensils	Pots and pans
Crock-type pot	Punch bowl
Cutting boards	Serving bowls
Eating utensils	Serving platters
Espresso makers	Serving utensils
Extension cords	Tables
Garbage cans	Tents/umbrellas
Hand truck/dolly	

Chapter 25

Chafing Dish —
What the Heck Is It and
What Can You Do with It?

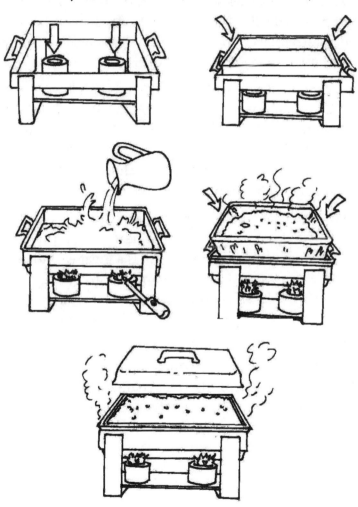

Definition

Here's one dictionary definition of a chafing dish:

chaf·ing dish \ `chaf-ing dish\ n : Used to maintain temperatures of food.

A chafing dish has several parts: the water pan, an insert pan, and a lid. Typically, a chafing dish comes in stainless steel, silver, copper, or even disposable aluminum. Its purpose is to maintain the temperature of cooked food.

A chafing dish is a unit with two levels: a lower-level pan that contains water and an upper-level compartment that contains the food. The heating source component looks a little like a candle inside a metal canister. There are many ways to heat a chafing dish, including candles, Sterno® canned heat, and electricity.

Why is a chafing dish so invaluable? Well, for one thing, it can help to keep your buffet areas neat. Also, if your event is outdoors, the lid on a chafing dish is a great way to keep bugs away from your food. Most important, chafing dishes can eliminate time and effort in maintaining food temperature, both hot and — as you'll learn here — cold.

If you're planning to host a lot of gatherings, you may want to invest in a chafing dish. Otherwise, try to borrow what you need. You can also rent chafing dishes from various party or catering supply stores. Some grocery and department stores carry inexpensive versions.

Using a Chafing Dish for Hot Food

Preheat larger food quantities on the stove or in the oven, and then transfer them into the chafing dish. The heating source for a chafing dish doesn't cook food — it simply keeps it hot.

- You can prepare a dish in the insert pan so long as the pan fits in your oven and is oven safe.

- If you're planning to hold food for an extended period of time, keep the lid in place to retain moisture.

- Never place anything flammable around the base of a hot chafing dish, such as decorations. Dried flowers will go up in flames pretty quickly!

- Most people know that a chafing dish is a warming apparatus, but the handles sometimes get really hot! After burning my hand a dozen or so times, I finally learned to use a cloth napkin. Run it through the eye of the handle and tie a knot in it. Then, for added decoration, you can put a rose through it.

Using a Chafing Dish for Cold Food

Another great way to use a chafing dish is to keep cold food items cold.

- Put ice in the water pan where you would ordinarily put hot water and, of course, don't bother using the heating source.

127

For a nice decorative touch, when placing cold food items inside, line the dish with lettuce or flowering kale.

You can also decorate the outside by wrapping a nice piece of fabric around the base. (But remember, this is a decorating tip for a **cold** chafing dish **only**, not a hot one.)

Lesser-known Uses for a Chafing Dish

Most people who have used a chafing dish are aware that it can be used for such foods as entrees, casseroles, vegetables, potatoes, and pastas. Here are some other ways to use a chafing dish:

Hot

Bread warmer/tortilla warmer
Sake (Japanese rice wine) warmer

Cold

Deli meats and cheeses
Desserts
Fresh fruit
Variety of salads
Vegetable display with savory dips
Dressing holder (leave dressing in bottles or place into a crock with a ladle and add ice to water pan)

Cleaning Your Chafing Dish

Before you use a chafing dish for the first time (whether you're using it for hot or cold food), wash it in soapy water, then rinse and dry it.

Regulate the burner under the chafing dish and check the water level in the lower pan periodically so that it doesn't burn dry. Also, don't preheat the dish without water.

When cleaning your chafing dish, do not use harsh cleaners, scouring pads, or steel wool.

To remove dried-on or burnt food, mix a couple of teaspoons of a nonabrasive cleanser with a couple of teaspoons of baking soda and water. Let it sit with the heating source underneath it for about 20 minutes until it begins to simmer. Then let the pan cool, rinse it, and dry it.

Depending on what your chafing dish is made of, you may want to clean the exterior with a silver, stainless steel, copper, or aluminum cleaner. This not only cleans food residue but also removes tarnish that might occur after overheating.

Heating Sources: Using Sterno® with Your Chafing Dish

Generally, you should have just above an inch of water when using a hot chafing dish.

Many heating sources allow you to regulate the temperature in order to maintain the level of warmth you want.

No matter which kind of heating source you choose, always wear hand protection, such as oven mitts, when you're handling the burner.

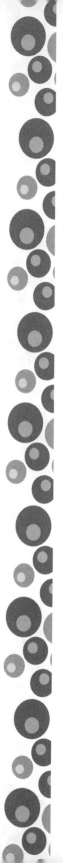

There are many types of heating sources, including canned fuels, solid heating gels, alcohol fuels, and burner cartridges. Here is information from the makers of Sterno®.

What is Sterno® Gel product made of?
Sterno® gel is a formulation of denatured alcohol, water and gel. It is perfectly safe when used as directed.

What happens if the gel is consumed internally? If Sterno® is ingested, please immediately call Poison Control at 888-313-8954. A medical specialist will advise you of the appropriate course of action. This number is staffed by certified medical professionals and is for MEDICAL EMERGENCIES ONLY. Alternately, you may seek medical attention.

Can food be prepared directly over the flame?
Although the emissions will not cause harm, it is not recommended. Certain foods may drip or burn and cause dangerous flare-ups resulting in bodily harm or damage to property. Do not attempt to eat any food that has fallen into the can or may have gel product on it.

How long does Sterno® burn? The 8 oz. can burns consistently or in increments equal to 2½ hours. The 2.6 oz. can burns consistently or in increments equal to 45 minutes. The gel is extinguishable and can be re-lit without affecting product performance.

How long can I keep Sterno® on my shelf?
It is recommended replacing Sterno® gel
product two years after purchase. Always
replace cover when not in use. Sterno® is
made partly of denatured alcohol which
evaporates from prolonged exposure to air.

The flame is blue, is that normal? The flame
from an alcohol mixture is normally blue and
sometimes invisible. Always assume a flame
is present until properly extinguished (see can
label). Safe handling procedures should
always be used when lighting and re-lighting.

Chapter 26

Ovens and Microwaves

Using the Oven and Microwave

Calibrate your oven's temperature. As ovens get older, the temperature tends to vary. If the thermometer in your oven says 400 degrees but you have your oven set to 450 degrees, it's time to call someone to calibrate it.

Measure your oven. Just try fitting a full-sized cookie sheet in a small apartment-sized oven, and you'll understand why this is important. Especially if your guests will be bringing food that needs to be cooked or heated, make sure your oven can accommodate everything.

Don't peek. Every time you check on your food by opening the oven door, the temperature drops as much as 25 degrees. If you want to peek, use that little oven light!

Follow the recipe. If the recipe says you should cook the food for 20 minutes at 250 degrees, don't cook it for 10 minutes at 500 degrees. If too high a setting is used, food may burn on the bottom before it's completely cooked.

Use a thermometer. Make sure it's an oven-safe model.

Never place pans on the floor of the oven. Pans should always be placed on a rack. The heat on the bottom is too concentrated, and it will burn the bottom of your food.

Keep dry foods moist. Put a pan of water on the bottom rack of the oven.

Keeping Your Oven Clean

For a spill in the oven, try sprinkling salt on it immediately and wipe it away once the oven has cooled.

To clean the plates under the elements of your stovetop, pop them into your self-cleaning oven when you clean it.

A paste made of baking soda and hot water makes a great oven cleaner. Just sponge it onto the stains and wipe clean.

Microwave Ovens – Do's and Don'ts

Knowing your microwave wattage is important. It can range from 500 to approximately 1200 watts; most microwave recipes are cooked at 700 watts. Here are a few microwave do's and don'ts.

Do's

Do read package instructions carefully. It's like a map — you can't get to the right place if you don't follow the directions.

Do place cooking bags on a microwave-safe plate and cut a slit in the bag's center. Otherwise, pressure will build up and the bag may burst.

Do poke holes in foods like potatoes. Without this "vent," they can explode.

Do keep your microwave oven clean. Drips and messes can slow cooking time or cause food to cook unevenly.

Don'ts:

Don't use non-microwave-safe plastic wrappings. They will melt and "bleed" dangerous materials into your food.

Don't use non-microwave-safe containers. The containers as well as the microwave may be damaged.

Don't close the container lid completely; it can cause the food to burst out of the container.

Don't add an extension cord to the microwave's factory-provided cord. This can cause sparks and an overloaded circuit.

Don't put any type of metal or reflective object in the microwave. This will cause sparks and potentially a fire.

Don't run other appliances from the same circuit as the microwave. If it doesn't cause an overload, it can very well cause reduced power flow to your

microwave, thus changing its cooking temperature. (See Chapter 8 "Electrical Power and
Circuits – Don't Overload Them" for more tips.)

Chapter 27

Buffets — How to Design and Set Them Up Effectively

Buffet Basics

🍽 What goes on the buffet? Plates, napkins, utensils, and food. Decorating your buffet is a great idea, but make sure you have room for your essential items.

🍽 If you're having just one main dish and a few side dishes, you may be able to use one large buffet table. However, if you're having a lot of different types of food, consider setting up the buffet tables as food stations throughout your venue. At one station, you might have appetizers. At another, entrées. At another, salads. At another, warm side dishes. And finally, the dessert.

🍽 Put all your cold food together — salads, chilled pastas, and so on. Similarly, put all your hot foods together.

🍽 Always serve your cold food first on the buffet. You'll want your guests to choose their cold foods and then decide on their hot foods. This ensures their hot foods won't get cold by the time they walk back to their tables.

If you don't have much of one particular buffet item, put it on the end of your buffet. That way people will fill their plates with the items of which you have plenty, then just a taste of the item of which you have little.

Don't forget the condiments such as mustard, chutney, or relish. If you have the room, set up a separate, smaller condiment table. This moves people away from the buffet so they're not blocking other's access to the food.

In order to make the party run smoothly so you're not running around, put out the desserts that don't require refrigeration at the same time you open your buffet. A separate table is recommended, unless you're pressed for space or dessert is a surprise.

Make coffee before you serve the food. You'd be amazed how many people like coffee with their meal.

Decorating the Buffet

You don't necessarily have to buy all the decorations for a buffet table. Here are some very simple and inexpensive items you can use to decorate your buffet, a few of which you might already have around the house.

Flowering kale. This species of the kale family, also known as flowering cabbage, has attractive white and creamy-yellow leaves and is readily available at supermarkets.

- **Greens and individual flowers.** Set out some floral greens and lay the open flowers on top.

- **Horsetail.** These thin, green, bamboo-like shoots are great to mix with flowers and are long lasting.

- **Leather leaf.** This is a type of fern you can purchase from your florist. Place a flower or two on top of each one.

- **Lemon leaf.** This looks like a smaller version of a lemon tree leaf. It's a filler plant over which you'd set some flowers.

- **Cutting boards.** These are great tools to display breads or carved meats. Make sure they're clean and free of bacteria.

- **Items from around the home.** Use toy or model cars for a party with an antique car theme. Use toy bear figurines for a children's birthday party. Place a long mirror on the tabletop. Set up potted plants around the table or on the tabletop to fill out a slightly bare buffet. Just about anything around your home can be turned into a decorative item.

- **Items from the backyard.** As long as they're not poisonous, bring in plants from your yard. (Wash them thoroughly to avoid bringing insects inside.) Other items from the yard that will help with the theme, such as a wagon wheel or statuette, could be placed on or around your buffet.

- **Risers.** You can make a riser out of a simple box. If it's too deep, cut it in half. For simple elegance, place fabric over the risers to create a flowing appearance.

❀ **Props.** Purchase (or borrow) items that will highlight your theme.

❀ **Lights.** Dig out some of those holiday lights to brighten your buffet.

Again, be sure to keep your decorative items away from chafing dish heating sources.

Buffet Placement

⚑ Walk the area that you intend to use for the party during the same time of day or night that you're planning to have the party. Keep in mind time changes. This will help you take into account considerations such as areas with heavy sunlight that will need to be shaded, or areas that will need more lighting at night.

⚑ If the buffet is outdoors, the best place for it is 10–15 feet from your back door. This puts you close enough to the kitchen to carry items outside and build your buffet.

⚑ Don't set up your buffet by an entrance, exit, or steps.

⚑ Don't set up your buffet near the dog run.

⚑ Don't place your buffet close to a patio or deck edge.

Chapter 28

Buffet Organization

The PartyCharlie 1-2-3 Buffet Setup

*I know it sounds like a dance step, but believe me,
if you follow this, you will have time to dance!*

Below is a blank **PartyCharlie 1-2-3 Step-by-Step Buffet Setup.** As you move through the steps, you'll fill out each stage to ensure that there's room for everything on your buffet and that everything looks great!

MENU ITEMS	SERVING EQUIPMENT NEEDED	ADDED TO DIAGRAM

Now you're ready to start with Step 1.

Step 1

In the left-hand column of the planning chart, list all menu items, plates, cutlery, napkins, floral centerpiece, and table decorations you'll have on your buffet.

Example:

- Soup: Minestrone
- Salads: Caesar salad
- Breads: Garlic bread
- Main courses: Lasagna and herb-roasted chicken
- Side dish: String beans
- Condiments: Parmesan cheese, chicken gravy
- Desserts: Fresh fruit slices and cake
- Plates
- Cutlery
- Napkins
- Floral centerpiece or table decorations

Here's what the PartyCharlie 1-2-3 Step chart looks like with Step 1 information filled in. We'll get to the other steps next.

Step 1 MENU ITEMS	SERVING EQUIPMENT NEEDED	ADDED TO DIAGRAM
Minestrone soup		
Caesar salad		
Garlic bread		
Lasagna		
Herb-roasted chicken		
String beans		
Parmesan cheese		
Chicken gravy		
Fresh fruit		
Cheesecake		
Plates		
Cutlery		
Napkins		
Floral centerpiece		

Step 2

In the column next to each menu item, list everything you'll need to serve your menu items. Knowing what serving bowl, platter, basket, chafing dish, etc., you're putting the food **in** or **on** will tell you how much room you'll need on your buffet table. This way, on the day of your event, you won't have to scramble for an additional table or — even worse — your buffet won't end up looking bare. Depending on your menu, this could include items such as these:

- Chafing dishes
- Tureens
- Casserole dishes
- Platters
- Compartment servers
- Serving bowls
- Punch bowls
- Crocks
- Serving spoons
- Condiment spoons
- Ladles
- Ice cream scoops
- Serving tongs
- Serving forks
- Carving knives
- Cheese knives
- Butter knives
- Cake server
- Spatulas
- Bread basket
- Plates
- Cutlery
- Napkins
- Floral centerpiece or table decorations

Now that you're done with Step 2, your chart will start to look like this.

MENU ITEMS	Step 2 SERVING EQUIPMENT NEEDED	ADDED TO DIAGRAM
Minestrone soup	Soup tureen & soup ladle	
Caesar salad	Salad bowl/tongs	
Garlic bread	Bread basket	
Lasagna	Chafing dish/spoon	
Herb-roasted chicken	Chafing dish/spoon	
String beans	Bowl/spoon or tongs	
Parmesan cheese	Bowl/spoon	
Chicken gravy	Gravy boat or bowl/ladle	
Fresh fruit	Platter or bowl/tongs or fork	
Cheesecake	Platter/cake server/cake knife	
Plates	Place in beginning of buffet	
Cutlery	Basket	
Napkins	Basket	
Floral centerpiece	Vase	

Step 3

Now that you know what you're putting your food, utensils, floral, etc., in or on, you'll know how much space you'll need.

Draw a diagram of your buffet based on the size of the table you're using. You don't have to draw the diagram to scale, although if you have the time and desire, that can make your planning more precise. Sketch out where on your buffet table(s) you will place your items.

🏳 Remember to sketch in your plates, eating utensils, and any floral arrangements or decoration items you're planning to include, because they will take up space.

🏳 Check off each item on your chart as you draw it on your diagram. That way you'll know you've addressed it.

Don't worry what your artwork looks like — even if it's not to scale, you'll still have a good planning tool when you're done.

When you're done with Step 3, your chart will look something like this:

MENU ITEMS	SERVING EQUIPMENT NEEDED	Step 3 ADDED TO DIAGRAM
Minestrone soup	Soup tureen & soup ladle	X
Caesar salad	Salad bowl/tongs	X
Garlic bread	Bread basket	X
Lasagna	Chafing dish/spoon	X
Herb-roasted chicken	Chafing dish/spoon	X
String beans	Bowl/spoon or tongs	X
Parmesan cheese	Bowl/spoon	X
Chicken gravy	Gravy boat or bowl/ladle	X
Fresh fruit	Platter or bowl/tongs or fork	X
Plates	Place in beginning of buffet	X
Cutlery	Basket	X
Napkins	Basket	X
Floral centerpiece	Vase	X

It's best to place your beverages in a separate location. Separating the food and beverages will increase the flow of your party or event. But if you need to include your beverages on the buffet table, make sure you include cups, ice, beverage garnishes, wine/bottle openers, and cocktail napkins.

Congratulations! You just learned The PartyCharlie 1-2-3 Step.

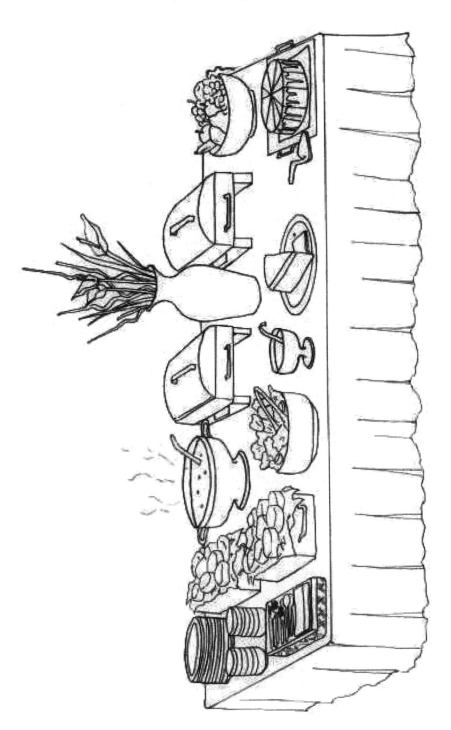

Buffet Table Setup

Chapter 29

Bars — Full Service

*I*n a full-service bar, you provide mixed drinks as well as wine, beer, champagne, and possibly after-dinner drinks (cordials). At a full-service bar, a bartender prepares and serves the drinks. You can hire help from a party staffing or catering company.

The first goal in setting up a bar is to make sure it's in the right place. Don't cause a bottleneck at the bar by placing it too close to the buffet, entrance, exit, guest tables, or restroom (unless the bar is permanent and you don't have a choice). Don't be afraid to place the bar at the far end of your party space. In fact, it will encourage guests to move farther into the party.

Next, figure out how much alcohol to provide. Estimate by considering what kind of alcohol you're serving and — again — remember the number 1 PartyCharlie rule: **Know your crowd.**

Making Your Bar Work

Before you can set up the bar, you're going to need a bar! If you don't have one, you can rent it. And don't forget the back bar — that's the table behind the bar, which acts as a supply station. You can use a table for the bar as well as the back bar if you'd rather not rent.

Your washing machine is a great backup for keeping your canned beverages on ice. It has its own draining system and is ready to go.

- Y A full-service bar can get expensive, but by estimating how much alcohol you'll need, you can keep costs to a minimum.

- Y To find out the trendy drinks in your area, contact local clubs or bars.

- Y Know your crowd. For instance, if it's a younger crowd, chances are that they won't be drinking scotch on the rocks.

- Y Hire a bartender. Your bartender will pour the right quantities, and alcohol won't be wasted.

Hosting a Cash Bar

- Y It's illegal to sell alcohol without a license even at your own house. Temporary liquor licenses are available for a fee. Check your city and state ordinances.

- Y Use drink tickets instead of having a bartender handle cash. Make sure your ticket person is very visible and has lots of change.

- Y Charge in whole dollar amounts (for instance, $3.00 instead of $3.50).

Benefits of Having a Bartender

- Y Bartenders will set up and break down the bar station.

- Y Bartenders will maintain the bar and keep the drinks cold.

Y Bartenders will take care of spills and broken glasses.

Y Bartenders have knowledge of different drink recipes for your guests to enjoy.

Y Bartenders will pour the right quantities, and alcohol won't be wasted.

Y The bartender will be constantly watching to make sure that the guests aren't drinking too much. You can have the bartender alert you to any over-intoxication problems, and then you can handle them discreetly. If the inebriated guest has a ride from a designated driver, be sure to inform the bartender.

Y The bartender will not serve drinks to minors.

Y When hiring a bartender, confirm that your bartender has a kit containing all the tools: shakers, pour tops, wine openers, ice tubs, etc.

A Reminder About Having a Bartender

If your party is at your home, it's up to you to decide whether you'll allow a "tip jar." If you don't allow one, find out if the bartender will be adding a gratuity cost to your bill.

Bottom line: If you don't want your guests to feel they have to tip, tell your bartender not to put out a tip jar. I personally do not permit bartenders to do so.

What You'll Need for a Wine and Beer Bar

This is the kind of bar I recommend if you're doing self-service. Anything more can get very complicated and end up sucking away all your time from mingling. Here's what you'll need:

- Wine, beer, champagne, water, and soft drinks

- Wine glasses or clear 10-ounce plastic tumblers

- Cocktail napkins

- Corkscrew/bottle opener

- Containers for soft drinks, wine, beer, and champagne and ice to keep them cold

- Ice bucket and scoop

- Trash bin with doubled or extra-strength trash bags

- Recycling bin for empty bottles and cans

What You'll Need for a Complete Bar

If you're having a complete bar and you plan on inviting more than 50 guests, **please** consider hiring a bartender. A self-service bar can get messy with that many people. But if you're feeling adventurous (and you have help), here's what you'll need for a complete bar:

Liquor/1 Liter Bottles

- Bourbon
- Cognac/Brandy
- Gin
- Rum – Light and/or Dark
- Scotch
- Tequila
- Triple Sec
- Vermouth – Dry
- Vermouth – Sweet
- Vodka
- Vodka – Flavored
- Whiskey
- Beer – Cans or Bottles
- Beer – Light – Cans or Bottles
- Wine – Red
- Wine – White

Juices/Quart Bottles:

- Cranberry juice
- Grapefruit juice
- Orange juice
- Pineapple juice
- Pomegranate juice

Party Planning Secrets

Carbonated mixers/1 Liter Bottles
- 7-Up or Sprite
- Club soda
- Cola
- Diet 7-Up or Sprite
- Diet Cola
- Ginger ale
- Sparkling Water
- Tonic water

Noncarbonated mixers/Various Sizes
- Bitters
- Bloody Mary mix
- Coconut milk
- Cream/milk
- Grenadine
- Lime juice
- Margarita mix
- Plain water
- Sour mix/Sweet & sour mix
- Tabasco sauce

Garnishes
- Cherries – maraschino
- Cinnamon sticks*
- Cocktail onions
- Cocktail picks
- Green olives – large
- Lemons & limes
- Melon cubes or balls*
- Mint leaves

- Orange wheels*
- Pineapple wedges*
- Specialty garnishes*
- Stuffed olives*
- Sugar, salt, and pepper*

Optional – used for specialty drinks and garnishes

Here is the type of equipment you should consider for your bar:

- Bar spoon (a long-handled spoon for mixing drinks and stirring in fruit)
- Bar/hand towels
- Blender
- Bottle opener
- Bowls for garnishes
- Can opener (church key)
- Cocktail shaker and strainer (to prevent ice from getting into non-iced drinks such as martinis and Old Fashioneds)
- Corkscrew
- Cutting board and sharp knife
- Ice bucket and scoop (for putting ice in drinks)
- Ice tongs
- Jars/cups to display garnishes
- Juice squeezer
- Measuring cups and spoons
- Pitcher for mixing larger amounts of drinks
- Stirrers
- Frilled toothpicks for bar garnish

Quantity Buying Suggestions

The general guideline on beverage quantities is to estimate two beverage servings per person for the first hour and one beverage serving per person per hour thereafter. For example, if you're hosting a four-hour party, you'll need to plan on approximately five beverage servings per person over the duration of the party.

Knowing your crowd will help you decide how to split the quantity of alcoholic and nonalcoholic beverages to serve. If you're unsure, a 50/50 split is usually safe. If you're concerned about purchasing too much alcohol, find a store that has a return policy for unopened bottles and cans. Many do, but be sure to ask first.

For a full-service bar, I recommend the quantities on the next page. If you're setting up a specialty bar such as a margarita or martini bar, you'll need approximately 25 percent more of the liquor for the featured drink.

A 750 milliliter bottle is approximately 25 ounces. A liter is approximately 33 ounces. A 1.5 liter is approximately 50 ounces. A typical shot is 1.5 ounces of liquor. If you really want break it down, here's how many 1.5-ounce shots you can get from the following:

Number of Bottles	1	2	4	6	12
750 milliliter	16	33	67	101	202
1 liter	22	45	90	135	270
1.5 liter	33	67	135	202	405

Suggestion: It's a nice touch to serve after dinner cordials, such as Bailey's, Amaretto and Grand Marnier, with coffee.

	25 Guests	50 Guests	100 Guests	200 Guests
Liquor/1 liter bottles				
Bourbon	1	1	1	2
Cognac/brandy	1	1	1	2
Gin	1	1	2	3
Rum – light and/or dark	1	1	1	2
Scotch	1	1	2	3
Tequila	1	1	2	3
Triple Sec	1	1	1	2
Vermouth – dry	1	1	1	2
Vermouth – sweet	1	1	1	2
Vodka	1	2	3	6
Vodka – flavored	1	1	2	3
Whiskey	1	1	1	2
Beer	½ case	1 case	1 ½ case	3 cases
Beer – light	½ case	1 case	1 ½ case	3 cases
Wine – red, 750 milliliter bottles	3	6	12	18
Wine – white, 750 milliliter bottles	3	6	12	18
Juices/Quart Bottles				
Cranberry juice	2	3	4	8
Grapefruit juice	1	2	3	4
Orange juice	2	3	6	8
Pineapple juice	1	1	2	3
Pomegranate juice	1	2	3	4
Carbonated Mixers/1 liter bottles				
7-Up or Sprite	2	4	6	8
Club Soda	2	3	4	8
Cola	2	4	6	8
Diet 7-Up or Sprite	2	4	6	8
Diet Cola	2	4	6	8
Ginger Ale	2	4	6	10
Sparkling Water	2	4	6	8
Tonic Water	3	6	8	10

Party Planning Secrets

	25 Guests	50 Guests	100 Guests	200 Guests
Noncarbonated Mixers/Various Sizes				
Bitters, small bottle	1	1	1	2
Bloody Mary mix, 1 liter	1	2	3	3
Coconut milk	*	*	*	*
Cream/milk	*	*	*	*
Grenadine, small bottle	1	1	1	2
Lime juice, small bottle	1	1	2	4
Margarita mix, 1 liter	1	2	4	8
Plain water, 1 liter	6	12	18	36
Sour mix/sweet & sour mix, 1 liter	1	2	3	6
Tabasco sauce, small bottle	1	1	1	2
Garnishes				
Cherries – maraschino	1 jar	1 jar	1 jar	2 jars
Cinnamon sticks	*	*	*	*
Cocktail onions	1 jar	1 jar	1 jar	2 jars
Cocktail picks	1 jar	1 jar	2 jars	4 jars
Green olive – large	1 jar	1 jar	2 jars	4 jars
Lemons ~ limes	3 ~ 6	6 ~ 12	9 ~ 18	18 ~ 36
Melons cubes or balls	*	*	*	*
Mint leave	1 bunch	1 bunch	1 bunch	1 bunch
Orange wheels	*	*	*	*
Pineapple wedges	*	*	*	*
Stuffed olives	*	*	*	*
Sugar, salt, and pepper	*	*	*	*
*optional – used for specialty drinks & garnishes				

These breakdowns are for 5-ounce servings of wine and champagne. Keep in mind that if you're using a larger wine glass, there will be fewer servings per bottle.

Number of Bottles	1	2	4	6	12
750 milliliter	5	10	20	30	60
1 liter	6	13	27	40	81
1.5 liter	10	20	40	60	121
3 liter	20	40	81	121	243

Types of Measuring Devices

Y **The double jigger.** This looks like two shot glasses placed end to end. Each half has a different measure — one is ¾ ounce and the other is 1½ ounces (known as one "jigger"). There are 1- and ½-ounce versions as well (known as a "pony").

Y **Shot glass, graduated.** This is a shooter with marks for ½- through 1½-ounce measures and can be used in place of a pony measure.

Y **Speed pourers.** These are spouts that fit over the ends of bottles. They're great for getting a steady, measurable pour, and they prevent drips and spills. A one-second count is equal to ½ ounce poured. Some pourers measure a proper shot so you won't have to count (known as a "3-ball liquor pour").

Non-alcoholic Beverage Stations

Generally, a nonalcoholic beverage serving over ice is 6 ounces. One can of soda is two servings. One liter is approximately five servings.

Here are just a few nonalcoholic beverages you can offer at your self-service station:

Y Cider

Y Cocoa

Y Fruit punch

Y Hot teas

Party Planning Secrets

Y Iced teas, including green, herbals, and fruit
flavored

Y Imported sparkling water with fruit wedges

Y Juices

Y Lemonade

Y Mineral water

Y Seltzer

Y Sodas

Y Spring water

Y "Virgin" (nonalcoholic) drinks such as margaritas,
daiquiris, and piña coladas

Chapter 30

Bars and Beverage Stations — Self-Service and Bartending Yourself

*L*abor can be expensive. For a small gathering, self-service bars are an economical alternative to a full-service bar. Below are some tips for setting up the bar the *PartyCharlie* way so everything you need is convenient. (See diagrams at end of this chapter.)

The Golden Rule for Self-Service Bars

Someone needs to keep an eye on the alcohol. This way you can make sure the area is kept clean and, more important, ensure that little guests aren't helping themselves to their first glass of wine. Sometimes children will find their way over to the bar to experiment, and while the adults are sitting around having a great time, they don't notice until too late that somebody has the hiccups.

Being the Bartender for Your Own Event

Handling the bartending yourself can be a lot of fun and can certainly make you the center of attention at the party. But keep in mind that it's also a lot of work. You may not have time to talk with your guests as much as you'd like, and it's harder to pay attention and handle other party details, such as making sure the food is replenished. So if you're going to bartend at your own party, plan in advance to have one, two, or even three volunteers to step in and take turns.

- ⍦ Provide a few drink recipes that can be made with the liquor you're providing. This will allow your guests to have fun making their own drinks and trying new recipes.

- ⍦ Keep two small trash cans next to the bar, one for trash and one for recyclables. Be sure they're doubled-lined and that backup bags are stored in the bottom of the can for quick replacement.

- ⍦ Don't place the bar in areas that have high traffic or near tables, entrances, exits, or restrooms.

- ⍦ You can make jugs of specialty drinks ahead of time. Make up fun names for the drinks to go with the theme of the party. Your guests can serve themselves with a theme drink that involves only adding ice.

- ⍦ Never touch the inside or the rim of the glass. Pick it up by grasping it around the lower part of the glass.

- ⍦ Rinse shaker glasses and other bar tools after every drink so you don't mix liquor from one kind of drink into another one. Set up tubs with hot water for rinsing.

- ⍦ Don't use the same ice you used to chill the bottles and cans in drinks you mix. It's not sanitary.

- ⍦ Use tongs or an ice scoop to put ice in the drinks. This will help to prevent the spread of germs.

Y **Never, never, never** use a glass to scoop up the ice. Glasses can break and send shards of glass into the drinks.

Keep Your Bar Fun and Festive

Y **Have an ice bar** — a bar that's carved from solid ice and lit up in your favorite color. You can even have your company logo or other design etched into the front of the bar. Contact an ice–sculpting company or your local ice company.

Y **Encase your vodka/liquor bottles in ice.** Get some empty half-gallon milk cartons. Clean them out and cut off the tops. Place the vodka bottle or favorite spirit inside, leaving equal room on all sides. Fill the carton to the brim with water. If you like, add flowers or slices of fruit. Then put the container in the freezer. (Vodka doesn't freeze.) When it's frozen, peel away the carton and you have a bottle of vodka encased in decorative ice.

Y **Have an ice company deliver a large block of ice.** Hollow out liquor bottle–sized holes with a chisel or power tool. Slide your bottles inside the holes. Place the ice in a tub with a water hose for draining melted water.

Y **Decorate your bar with strands of lights.** Pull out those Christmas lights. Even if it's July, they can be a lot of fun.

Y **Use creative garnishes** — watermelon, pineapples, mango cubes, candies, and teardrop marinated tomatoes (in addition to the standbys: lemon, lime, oranges, and cherries).

Make It Easy on Yourself

☓ To keep things running smoothly, watch over the bar yourself or appoint one of your volunteers to do so.

☓ To save money on your bar, harken back to your college days and ask your guests to BYOB (bring your own booze). Then set up a nice self-service bar with all the accessories (glasses, napkins, stirrers, etc.).

☓ For fun and ease of use, you may want to post recipes on how to make the most common or popular drinks.

☓ If you're limiting your bar selection to wines, beers, and wine coolers, place the beverages in ice bins and position them around the party space along with plastic tumblers. Then be sure to replenish when necessary. This eliminates the need for a bar altogether. (P.S. Don't forget the bottle opener… tie it to the ice bin.)

The Setup

☓ Set up one beverage station for every 75 guests.

☓ Spread the stations around and place them away from entrances and exits so that bottlenecking is kept to a minimum.

⅄ Open the stations farthest from the entrance first. This will encourage guests to make their way farther into the venue.

⅄ Add a recycling and trash container for each station.

Coffee Service

See Chapter 31, "Coffee – Making Sense of the Many Choices" for tips on setting up coffee stations.

Soft Drink Service

Place the glasses or 10-ounce plastic tumblers at one end of the table, followed by ice with at least one scoop, then the soft drinks, cocktail napkins, and a recycling container for empty cans or bottles. It's also a good idea to store extra soft drinks under the table.

Basic Self Service Bar

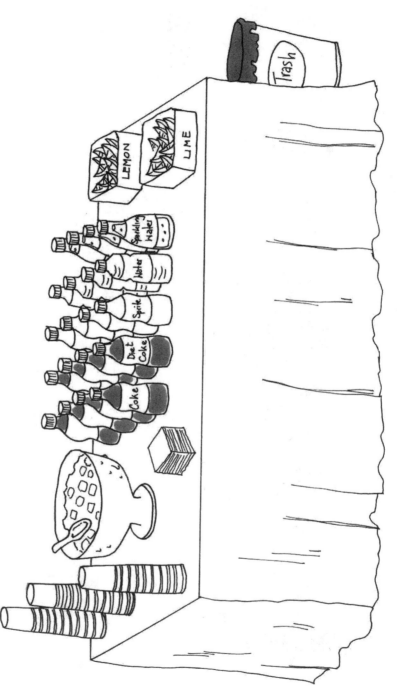

Soft Beverage Bar

Chapter 31

Coffee — Making Sense of the Many Choices

*F*or a great pick-me-up, coffee is one of the most fundamental elements to any great party or event. And yet it is often forgotten in the planning. Hosting a party is an enormous task, with food and alcoholic beverages being the top priority in the party giver's mind. This may be the biggest reason that coffee is overlooked. Or maybe it's sub-conscious, stemming from the anxiety of having to make a good cup of coffee for dozens of people. Fear not — I'm here to rescue you from your coffee worries forever!

PartyCharlie Coffee Tips

- When buying loose coffee beans, crack a bean between your fingernails. If it cracks easily and you smell the vibrant aroma, it's fresh. Old coffee is rubbery, will have a flat smell, and will sometimes give off a rancid odor.

- Purchase whole-bean coffee and grind it at the store. Do this a couple of days in advance. Great coffee will still be great a day or two after grinding.

- Keep your coffee as fresh as possible by storing it in an airtight container. Bag it and squeeze out the excess air. Store the coffee in a cool, dark place.

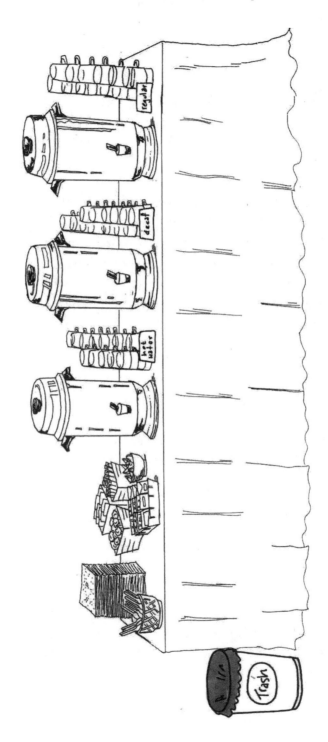

Self Serve Coffee Bar

Party Planning Secrets

Never freeze your opened coffee. In the freezer it is exposed to moisture, which will change the flavor.

A cup of coffee is only as good as the water used to make it. Always start with cold filtered or bottled water.

Use clean equipment. When oils get trapped inside the coffeemaker, the coffee you brew will contain unpleasant-tasting remnants. Running water through your filter will help keep it clean.

Large-capacity coffeemakers will reach temperatures between 180 and 200 degrees. Make sure to keep the unit clean. If it isn't clean, the thermostat will not sense the temperature correctly and the coffee will not be as hot as it should be.

It's always a good idea to provide decaffeinated along with regular coffee.

Be sure to indicate which coffee has caffeine and which is decaffeinated. One simple and creative way of doing this is by noting each on place cards using calligraphy.

If you're going to serve only one type of coffee, make it decaffeinated. Because of allergies or medical reasons, some of your guests might not be able to have caffeine.

Coffee condiments can help to make a good cup of coffee even better. For a little extra flair, you can also provide creamers, fun flavorings, and an assortment of spices and sweeteners for your coffee bar, such as cinnamon, nutmeg, mocha, and vanilla.

How Many Cups Will You Need?

☕ Plan on one cup of coffee per adult guest. Some people will have two, and others won't have any at all.

☕ Once you determine how many cups you'll need, rent or borrow the appropriate-sized coffeemaker — either a 25-cup, 50-cup, or 100-cup maker.

☕ Coffeemakers come with instructions, but if those instructions are lost, just look inside and follow the little notches indicating how much water you should add in order to make the number of cups you want.

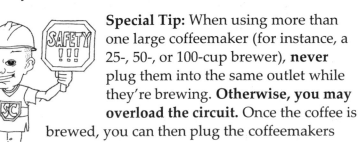

Special Tip: When using more than one large coffeemaker (for instance, a 25-, 50-, or 100-cup brewer), **never** plug them into the same outlet while they're brewing. **Otherwise, you may overload the circuit.** Once the coffee is brewed, you can then plug the coffeemakers into the same outlet. They utilize less power when the brewing process has been completed.

Coffee Percolator Instructions

1. **Fill with water.**
Remove the cover and basket. Fill with fresh, **cold** filtered or bottled water to the cup mark desired. Never use hot water. **Do not** fill the coffeemaker above the highest cup mark.

2. Measure coffee.

Wet the coffee basket to keep small coffee particles from sifting through the basket. Place the basket on the stem. Be sure that the bottom of the percolator cube is fitted properly in the heating well. Add **regular grind** coffee according to the chart below.

I'll make it easy for you to calculate the quantity of coffee to use for the number of servings. I use the most common rule of thumb, which is 1 ½ tablespoons of coffee per cup. You can vary this amount depending on your personal taste. You can usually buy coffee in 12 and 16 ounce bags.

25 drink cups	approx. 18 ounces	2¼ measuring cups of coffee
50 drink cups	approx. 36 ounces	4½ measuring cups of coffee
100 drink cups	approx. 72 ounces	9 measuring cups of coffee

NOTE:
1 cup of coffee = 6 fluid ounces of water
1 measuring cup = 8 ounces of coffee

3. Brewing strength.

Coffee can be brewed to any strength desired by adding to or subtracting from the recommended amounts of coffee above.

4. Brewing.

Place the lid on the coffeemaker. Allow approximately 1 minute per cup brewing time. This may vary due to changes in voltage and temperature. Plug the cord into any AC outlet with 110–120 voltage. On some makers, brewing begins automatically, and on others, you need to push a button. On some coffeemakers, when the signal light comes on, the coffee is ready to serve. On others, the light goes on to tell you the coffee is brewing. Just make sure you know what the light means.

All coffeemakers automatically switch to low heat after brewing and will keep coffee at proper serving temperature as long as they're plugged into an outlet.

5. Remove coffee grounds.
To maintain perfect flavor, remove the basket with coffee grounds as soon as the brewing stops.

Setting Up a Coffee Station

Set up coffee stations for quick service, placing the coffee cups at the beginning of the table, followed by regular coffee, decaf, tea bags, and hot water for tea. Be sure to identify each hot beverage with a sign. Don't forget the cream, sugar, artificial sweetener, spoons, and a small trash receptacle for used tea bags and trash.

Alternative Uses for a Coffeemaker

A coffeemaker can also be used for:

- ☕ Cocoa
- ☕ Hot tea
- ☕ Cider
- ☕ Hot toddies
- ☕ Cold beverages

Yes, you read that right — you can use a coffeemaker for cold beverages. Just remove the stem from the pot and place it somewhere you won't lose it. The inside should be cleaned well because it might still have a coffee smell or flavor that will get into your noncoffee beverage.

☕ If you're making a beverage from scratch, congratulations! If not, pour a powdered beverage mix, water and ice into the coffee pot. You then have a beverage container with a spigot.

☕ Make sure you put a card out that lists the contents in the coffee pot because otherwise everyone will assume it's coffee.

☕ **Do no**t use beverages with any pulp or fruit pieces because this will clog the spigot.

☕ This probably goes without saying, but if you're using the coffeemaker to hold a cold beverage, **don't plug it in.**

Espresso and Cappuccino Carts

A nice addition to your party is an espresso and cappuccino cart. Most vendors provide carts to serve a variety of drinks:

☕ Ice-blended coffee drinks

☕ Fresh fruit and juice smoothies

☕ Assorted iced blended drinks

☕ Assorted iced coffee drinks

☕ Hot cappuccinos

☕ Hot lattes

☕ Hot mochas

☕ Chai teas

Be sure you have access for the cart within the party space, and don't forget to designate a separate power line for the cart.

For additional information on renting espresso and cappuccino carts, refer to the PartyCharlie Vendor Questionnaire in Chapter 55 — PartyCharlie's Templates and Checklists.

Section 4

THE SMALL DETAILS THAT MAKE A BIG IMPACT

Chapter 32

Guests – Getting Them Involved

S tep 4 of my Five Steps to 'Create the Energy' for an Outrageously Exciting Party – "Involve Your Guests by Giving Them Something to Do."

As recommended in Step 2 of my Five Steps (see Chapter 3), for the benefit of your guests, you must have a greeter at the door for at least the first hour to welcome everyone who arrives. This lets them know that you appreciate their coming, and it's a great opportunity to tell them what's available at the function so they don't miss out on anything. Most of all, it gets their energy going!

Below are my most powerful PartyCharlie tips to ensure that your party is **outrageously exciting.**

30 Ways to Get Your Guests Involved

1. **Introduce your guests.** Introduce each guest to at least one other person who shares a common interest.

2. **Reduce your chairs.** At a cocktail party, always have fewer chairs than guests (have just enough for 25%–50% of the guests). This keeps your guests moving and the energy flowing as they mingle and circulate.

3. **Throw a potluck.** This is a natural way to involve your guests because they will be making a contribution to the party the moment they walk in the door.

4. **Provide name tags.** It may sound a little hokey, but this is a great way for people to feel comfortable introducing themselves to other guests.

5. **Host a wine tasting.** This is a wonderful way for guests to mingle.

6. **Supply disposable digital cameras.** Provide cameras for your guests to take pictures. Collect them at the end of the party, and e-mail the best ones to the guests.

7. **Throw a theme party.** Theme parties and costumes are a fun way to get guests involved before they even show up at the party. See Chapter 10, "Theme – Selecting the Right One for Your Party," for more theme-related ideas.

8. **Hire a musician, DJ, or band.** This will provide entertainment and get people on the dance floor.

9. **Offer a dance lesson.** Hire a local ballroom or salsa teacher to come in and shake things up.

10. **Hold a freeze dance.** As the party gets going, gather a group of guests on the dance floor and have the DJ start the music. Then have him turn off the music at times during the song. Every time the music stops, the guests must freeze in position. The last person who freezes has to sit down. The final person left standing wins a prize. (This game can be fun for both children and adults.)

11. **Provide a karaoke machine.** Often the people who you'll hear making jokes about karaoke are the same

ones who are up at the microphone singing away at a party.

12. **Do makeovers.** Hire a makeup artist (or a team of them) to do makeovers for your guests.

13. **Hire a fortune teller.** This is a great way of entertaining your guests and encourages mingling as guests compare notes.

14. **Teach a craft at your party.** If you or one of your volunteers knows a craft, teach it to your guests. Don't forget to provide the supplies and protect the furniture with disposable table coverings.

15. **Award prizes.** Every 15 or 30 minutes, have the DJ call out a question that pertains to the guests at your party, such as: "Who's the youngest here?" "Who's wearing the best costume?" "Who brought the tastiest food?" Have the DJ award a prize to each winner.

16. **Hold a charades tournament.** Teams can battle one another in a fast-paced round of charades. The winners will play one another in the next round, and so on. Prizes are given at each stage, with a grand prize at the end. Depending on how many people are at your party, you can have anywhere from two to four rounds.

17. **Hold a board game tournament.** Set up a variety of board games, specifying a 15-minute time limit, and tell your guests that the winners of each game get a certain number of points. The person with the most points wins a prize. (If there's a tie, you can have a final face-off.)

18. **Throw a casino games night.** Rent casino-style games for use at your party. If it's a charity event, the "house winnings" can be donated.

19. **Have a carnival game party.** It's easy to set up carnival-type games such as water gun target practice, a coin toss, a pie-eating contest, and ring around the bottles.

20. **Offer lawn games.** Party rental companies offer some terrific, large-sized inflatable lawn games like a bounce house, dunking booth, and lawn bowling.

21. **Host an "Olympic games" party.** Set up your own prize-filled version of the Olympics, with games like flag football, horseshoes, three-legged race, egg toss, and water polo if you have a pool.

22. **Organize a scavenger hunt.** Provide lists to each of your guests and then allow them to form two-person teams. You can make it an elegant affair by providing champagne and asking the guests to dress in formal attire.

23. **Hire a magician.** A magician can be entertaining as well as a great medium for getting guests involved.

24. **Hire a caricaturist.** This is a way of involving your guests and treating them to a gift at the same time. They'll have fun comparing pictures.

25. **Hire a masseuse.** Neck and shoulder massages can be amazing stress relievers for a party that follows a hard day at work. And the more comfortable and

happy your guests are, the more likely they will be to want to get to know one another.

26. **Hold an interactive cooking party.** Have your guests bring an apron and their favorite food, and everyone can help one another prepare a dish. You supply the wine!

27. **Have a name game.** As your guests arrive at the party, tape the name of a famous person on everyone's back. As guests mingle, they can ask for clues about their famous person. When a guest announces the name on their back, they win a prize.

28. **Encourage conversation.** Place Trivial Pursuit cards in bowls where guests will see them. Encourage your guests to read the questions to one another to start conversations.

29. **Break the ice.** All those who wish to learn the names of the new friends get into the circle. Start by going clockwise, with each guest announcing his or her first and last name. Now the first person must try to name all the guests. If he or she misses, the next person takes over. You would be surprised how quickly this happens. And it gets funny!

30. **Promote curiosity.** Assign someone to walk around with a box with a gift in it. Give clues about what's in the box, but don't make it easy. Guests are not allowed to ask questions. Give a new clue every minute. Ask people to write their guess on a small piece of paper. If there is a tie, flip a coin!

Chapter 33

Volunteers — Making the Most of Them

*F*riends who have volunteered to assist at the party, can help you organize your party, lend and/or gather borrowed equipment, be there when the rental truck arrives, and so on. Here's how to make the most of them.

When You Need Help But Won't Ask a Guest

Ask for help! Here are a few reasons we say we don't need help:

1. We don't want our guests to feel as though they're "singing for their supper." Asking a guest to help with one small task can make a big difference, so don't be shy — ask!

2. We want everyone to think of us as Supermen and Superwomen who can put together a party for a hundred guests without any help at all.

3. We're sometimes afraid that when a friend asks if he or she can help, the guest is only doing so because it's an obligation rather than a sincere desire to be of assistance.

Party Planning Secrets

Here's what happens when you just say YES:

1. You get much-needed assistance.

2. Your guests get the pride of knowing they've helped you put together a great event.

3. Everyone who comes to the party enjoys how seamlessly and smoothly everything runs.

PartyCharlie Tips on Using Volunteers

🏳 **Recognize when you need help.** We all like to have the pride of doing things on our own, but putting together a party is a big endeavor (even with all my guidance and tips). So recognize when you're feeling a little overwhelmed, and rather than allowing yourself to burn out, turn to volunteers.

🏳 Use my **PartyCharlie Checklist** at the end of this book to determine in which areas you could use assistance.

🏳 Make a list of equipment you need to borrow and assign this task to a volunteer.

🏳 Make a list of the times when you expect rental deliveries, such as for tables and chairs. Don't forget that if you're allowing one of your volunteers to do this, he or she needs to check in every rental piece so you don't get charged for something that was damaged or never arrived.

Invite your volunteers to choose a job they would enjoy doing. People are more likely to do something well if they really care about it.

Thanking Your Volunteers

Acknowledge your volunteers. When guests tell you how great the party is, remember to give credit where credit is due.

At the very least, send a card to thank each volunteer.

You can also present a little gift bag to your volunteers.

If it's appropriate, deliver a short thank-you toast to acknowledge your volunteers at your party or event.

Chapter 34

Coat Check – Planning and Setting Up

Here are some tips on making sure your guests leave with the outerwear they came in with.

Informal Coat Check

☐ Set aside one room as the coat check room. For a limited number of guests, it's perfectly fine to neatly pile the coats on a bed if your coat closet is full.

☐ If you have many guests or you'd just like to have a more organized way of taking care of the coats, empty your hallway closets (for instance, put your own coats in a spare room) and post a sign on the closet doors indicating to guests that they can hang their coats inside.

☐ For a relatively low price, you can rent an expandable rolling coat rack with hangers and set it up in a room that won't be used for the party, or in an area that has little traffic. Contact your local party rental company for availability.

Formal Coat Check

☐ Catering, party rental, and party planning companies usually offer coat check services. The

coat check staff will be in charge of keeping track of the coats and getting them back to their rightful owners. If you're renting a room in a hotel or country club, find out if the coat check service costs extra or if it's included in the package.

☐ If you're holding a charity event and having a formal coat check, it's perfectly acceptable to recoup your costs from your guests. You can charge them anywhere from $1 to $3 per coat.

☐ If you're hosting a large cocktail or holiday party in your home, consider the cost of having a coat check as part of your party budget. You wouldn't expect to go to a friend's home and pay to hang up your coat.

☐ If your party is at home and you hire a coat check service, decide whether you'll allow a tip jar. As I mentioned in the chapter on bars, I don't allow tip jars. Find out if the coat check service provider will be adding a gratuity cost to your bill. If so, definitely don't allow the tip jar.

PartyCharlie Coat Check Tip

Whether or not you hire professionals to handle your guests' coats, a neat idea is to buy two matching decks of cards and punch holes in each. One of the cards will go to the guest and the other will be attached to the coat hanger.

Chapter 35

Trash — It Stinks, But You Have to Plan for It

PartyCharlie Trash Tips

You won't believe how much trash you'll accumulate during a four-hour party. Throwing the trash in your neighbor's pool is not an option, so here's how to plan in advance:

☐ Be sure to use heavy-duty bags and seal them tightly. You don't need to spend your time cleaning up the messes from broken trash bags.

☐ If your regular trash day happens to fall a day or two after your party, planning for the disposal will be easy.

☐ If your trash day is several days after the party, you may want to call the waste disposal company and find out if you can arrange for a special pickup and whether there is a charge.

☐ For larger parties, order extra trash bins from the waste disposal company.

☐ Keep extra trash bags in the bottoms of the cans. That way, when you dispose of one bag, you won't have to go searching for another.

☐ I recommend keeping lids off the trash cans. It will be easier for your guests to throw away their

187

disposable plates, napkins, and beverage tumblers.

When setting up trash cans outside, place some citronella candles or spray some insecticide around the rims of the cans. This will help to keep away flying insects and bugs, but don't place the candles too close to flammable items!

Don't leave your filled trash bags sitting out in the yard for several days after the party. This is a big temptation for neighborhood cats, dogs, and raccoons.

More Trashy Talk

If you're using an old, unattractive garbage can, consider buying wrapping paper and taping it around the outside of the can. The paper you choose can complement the theme of party.

If you don't want to go to the trouble of "gift wrapping" your old garbage can, put it **inside** a trash bag (a 55-gallon bag usually does the trick). Tape the trash bag over the edges of the can so it doesn't slip off. Then put in the trash liners as you ordinarily would. If it sounds complicated, it's not. Just check out the diagrams on the following page.

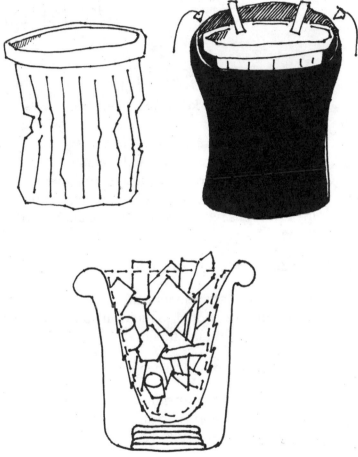

Chapter 36

Bathroom — Preparing It for the Party

PartyCharlie Tips

Here are a few tips to help keep smiles on your guests' faces.

- [ ] Keep several extra rolls of toilet paper in the bathroom. If you don't have a toilet paper rack specifically designed for this purpose, just place the extra rolls where guests can see and reach them.

- [ ] Use disposable decorative hand towels.

- [ ] Place a new air freshener near the toilets. Some types can be mounted to the wall and some stand discreetly behind the toilet.

- [ ] Keep a can of spray freshener handy.

- [ ] Provide some of those cute little wrapped soap bars, or keep liquid soap at the sink. (Most people will use liquid soap.)

- [ ] Put a box of tissues on the vanity counter or on the back of the toilet.

- [ ] If you have a medicine cabinet, remove all prescription drugs and anything else that could cause a problem if taken incorrectly. Some people have a habit of peeking in the medicine cabinet, and accidents happen.

☐ Place a small basket on the vanity containing such items as hand lotion, dental floss, mouthwash with small paper cups, breath strips, a travel-sized bottle of hair spray, and a small sewing kit.

☐ Keep a supply of sanitary napkins and tampons in a cabinet next to or under the sink.

☐ Fresh flowers and a small scented votive candle in a candle holder are nice touches. Be sure to set the vase in a place where it won't be knocked over and the candle in a place where it can burn safely.

☐ Keep a plunger near the toilet for emergencies. You can make it look a little nicer for the party by setting it on a doily and tying a ribbon around the handle.

☐ Check the bathrooms once an hour during the party to determine if anything needs to be restocked or to tidy up the area. If you can't do this yourself, assign a volunteer.

☐ Tuck a container of premoistened bathroom wipes under the sink to be used for any quick cleanups that may be necessary.

Chapter 37

Final PartyCharlie Planning Tips

☐ **Walkie talkies.** If you're having a large event and working with volunteers or a team, it's a good idea to rent walkie talkies. You'll find listings in the local phone book under "Two Way Radios" or "Walkie Talkies," or search the Internet for companies that rent them.

☐ **Smoking.** If you don't want people smoking inside, set some ashtrays outside. Just don't put the ashtrays anywhere near the food.

☐ **Lighting.** Make sure food areas are well lit.

☐ **Power/electrical.** Make sure you have adequate power. (More details are in Chapter 8, "Electrical Power and Circuits–Don't Overlook Them.")

☐ **Pets.** Make arrangements to send your pets to a kennel or to a friend's or family member's home. Don't burden your guests with having to hear "Close the door — don't let the dog/cat out!"

☐ **Gifts.** If guests will be bringing gifts, designate an area for them. Note that the gift area **should not** be close to the front door. Remember, even though you know who you're inviting, you don't know who *they're* inviting. Sometimes gifts have a funny way of walking away!

☐ **Freezer.** If your freezer has built up a two-inch layer of ice, it's time to defrost.

Party Planning Secrets

Storing foods. Purchase inexpensive food storage containers and zipper-style plastic bags that you can use to send leftover food home with guests.

Gifts for the guests. Give gifts to your guests. If you have a valet service, you can have the valet staff distribute the gifts to guests as they leave the party. Have the valet set up the gift table after everyone has arrived but early enough to accommodate guests who may be leaving early.

Babysitting. If the party is for adults only, plan on sending your kids to a babysitter. Send them for the whole day — not just for the party. Unless they're old enough to help you with last-minute preparations, letting them hang around before the party can get a bit stressful. If you can, arrange for the kids to be picked up by someone you trust rather than stopping your party prep to drop them off yourself.

Lawn parties. Stop watering the lawn two or three days in advance (unless it's incredibly dry) to give the ground time to harden. You don't want any guests' high-heeled shoes sinking in and risking a fall or twisted ankle. Also, soggy soil and grass will be damaged when your guests trample on it. Firm soil and grass will not be harmed. Make sure you turn off automatic sprinklers.

Wardrobe. Select your wardrobe a week before the party. If you haven't worn the outfit lately, try it on. Clothes have a funny way of shrinking

when they hang in the closet for long periods of time.

Dry cleaners. Make sure you have your clothing cleaned and picked up days before the event.

Delivery confirmations. Confirm any pickups and deliveries with your vendors a couple of days before the party and reconfirm on the actual day.

Prep in advance. Remember these famous last words: "It will only take a minute." There are many preparations to be handled. Don't leave things for the day of the party if you can do them earlier.

Section 5

THE DAY OF YOUR PARTY

Chapter 38

Go Hydrate and Get Yourself Something to Eat!!!

$\mathcal{R}$emember to hydrate and eat before the party. I cannot stress this enough. On the day of your party, your adrenaline will be running the show. Your system will be a little off. You'll have a lot of nervous energy. You won't want to eat, and you definitely won't be drinking water.

But please, even if you have to set an alarm clock, remember to have small healthy nibbles and drink water in the morning, afternoon, and an hour before the party. Here are just a couple of the scenarios I've witnessed over the years:

🍽️ I've seen hosts get weak from hunger before the party but keep going so they can say hello to all

the incoming guests. Then they stuff themselves with food, get a giant sugar rush, and have to leave their own party to go lie down for a while.

🍽 I've seen the host or hostess get very tipsy very quickly after not having eaten anything all day. Stay away from alcohol until your party starts, and do yourself a favor — don't get hammered!

So...

GO HYDRATE AND GET YOURSELF SOMETHING TO EAT!!!

The Day of Your Party

☐ **Hydrate.** Did I mention that you should hydrate and get yourself something to eat?

☐ **Babysitter.** Have the babysitter pick up the kids early in the day.

☐ **Pets.** Have a volunteer drop your pets at the kennel.

☐ **Smoking.** Set up ashtrays for your guests. If you don't want them smoking inside, put them outside away from the food areas.

☐ **Valuables.** Lock up your valuables and put away your breakables. Certainly you wouldn't invite your guests if they weren't trustworthy, but accidents happen.

☐ **Private.** Make sure any rooms that you don't want guests to enter are marked with a sign reading "Private. Please do not enter."

Party Planning Secrets

☐ **Gifts.** Set up the gift drop-off area, and remember not to place it near any entrances or exits.

☐ **Phone calls during the party.** If you don't want to answer the phone a dozen times before the party begins, record an outgoing message with directions to the party venue for folks who need them. (Don't do this if you have any concerns that you might wind up with unwanted guests.)

☐ **Getting dressed.** Get into your dress clothes about an hour before the party. If you follow my tips, you won't have to do any last-minute preparations, although you may want to do things like check over the buffet areas. Just be sure you don't get anything on your outfit.

☐ **Hygiene.** Brush your teeth before your guests arrive to ensure that you have clean and fresh-smelling breath.

☐ **Greet your guests.** As each guest comes in, greet him/her or have a greeter offer beverages and hors d'oeuvres to make him or her feel comfortable. Remember — high energy is the key!

☐ **Get your guests to mingle.** Introduce each guest to at least one other person who shares a common interest. If at all possible, try to find a common interest not business-related, such as a hobby. Most people don't want to talk about business at a party.

☐ **Allow your guests to talk.** Don't monopolize the conversation just because it's your party. Allow others to feel a part of the event. When in a

conversation with a group, pass the conversation over to a guest and let the person talk.

☐ **Meet all your guests.** Don't focus on just one person. Mingle! This will encourage your guests to do so as well.

☐ **Most important: HAVE FUN!!!**

Chapter 39

Guests Who Can't
or Won't Leave —
Prevention and Coping

Sometimes it can be hard to know when to cut off a
guest's bar privileges or take away the keys. After all, as
the host, you want everyone to leave having had a good
time. And if you follow these tips, you'll likely be able to
stop problem drinking before it starts.

- Be specific on your invitations. Especially if you
  aren't a person who likes to have a party go on
  into the wee hours, indicate an ending time. For
  example, "Please join us from 7 PM until 11 PM"
  is clear. Indicating "The party is from 7 PM until
  whenever" will give your guests a license to get
  too intoxicated to make it home.

- Circulate plenty of appetizers as soon as your
  guests arrive. This will help to ensure they don't
  drink on an empty stomach.

- As recommended in Step 4 of my "Five Steps to
  'Create the Energy' for an Outrageously Exciting
  Party" (see Chapter 3), give your guests
  something to do at the party (games, dancing,
  eating, etc.). This will help lead to more
  conversation, and people will be less likely to get
  hammered.

Make sure that anyone serving alcohol (whether a professional or volunteer) is of legal age and knows not to over pour the alcohol.

If you have a full-service bar, ask your bartender to let you know if he feels any guests are going a little overboard with the drinking. But **do not** instruct the bartender to handle it on his or her own. Chances are that if you speak with your guest, he or she will be more respectful to you than to your bartender.

If you have a self-service bar, keep an eye on your guests' drinking. Don't get so tipsy yourself that you can't tell if your guests have had too much to drink. Also, since you, as the host, are the focus of the evening, you'll likely not want everyone leaving the party discussing how drunk you were.

Offer lots of fun nonalcoholic drinks, such as fresh juice, punch, virgin drinks, fancy soft drinks, imported sparkling water, or my favorite — root beer!

If you have underage guests and a full-service bar, instruct your bartender to ask for ID.

If you have underage guests and a self-service bar, rotate volunteers (including yourself) and decide who will keep an eye on the area at any given time. Oh, and be sure your volunteers aren't underage!

Close the bar at least 30 minutes before the scheduled end of the party. At this point, serve only water, soft drinks, and coffee. You can also bring out additional desserts and snacks. This will give guests time to prepare to head home and will give you the opportunity to see if any of them need help getting home.

For our friends who have had a wee bit too much to drink, have a spare room ready or get them to a nearby hotel. **Do not let them drive.** You can be held legally liable if your guest hurts someone in a car accident.

Recognize the signs. If a guest is stumbling or slurring his words, **do not** let that person get behind the wheel.

You can also get a cab for an intoxicated guest, but **do not** put someone in a cab who is too drunk even to give directions to the cabbie.

Arrange for designated drivers before the party begins.

Know when to address medical emergencies. The National Council on Drug and Alcohol Dependence defines the signs of alcohol poisoning as cold, clammy, pale, or bluish skin and slow respiration. Call 911 immediately.

Bottom line: Be a responsible host. You have a moral and, in most states, a legal obligation to provide for your guests.

Hosts are being held accountable for the well-being of partygoers after they leave the party. You could be held responsible for damages and/or injuries that occur as the

result of the alcohol you serve your guests during the party. You are responsible for your guests' actions when they leave your home as a result of the party or event you hosted. The solution is to be a smart host as well as a good host.

Section 6

AFTER YOUR PARTY

Chapter 40

Rentals – Returning Them Properly and Avoiding Penalties

*H*ere are some tips on returning rentals.

☐ Just as you did when the rentals arrived, check all items before you return them or have them picked up by the rental company.

☐ Note any damaged items as well as the specific nature of the damage. Give a copy of this list to the delivery/pickup person and keep a copy for yourself. That way, you can be sure that there is no confusion over what was returned to the company.

☐ Return the items on time. Rental companies charge late fees for each day they don't get their equipment back because that's another day they can't rent it to other clients.

☐ Rinse your rentals. Rental companies charge a fee if plates, silverware and glasses are not rinsed.

Chapter 41

Cleanup – Making It a Little Less Dreadful

*L*et's face it, cleanup can be a drag no matter how many tips I give you. However, I can make it easier and help you to eliminate a lot of the hassle if you follow these suggestions.

- **Clean as you go.** After you've enjoyed yourself at your wonderful party and are so tuckered out that you just want to go to bed, it can be overwhelming to see a pile of dishes, pots, and pans in the kitchen. If you clean as you go, you'll feel a whole lot better about having invested so much time and effort in hosting a party.

- **Employ staff to continuously clean as the party is happening.** This will make a significant difference at the end of the event.

- **Teach your kids the value of money in exchange for hard work.** Prearrange with your kids to be in charge of the cleanup for a set price.

- **Have your volunteers help.** Again, prearrange this so it doesn't seem like a last-minute plea. For larger events and parties, make it fun by inviting your volunteers to a small brunch, a light snack, or some of the fabulous leftovers from the night before to thank them for their help.

Call a reputable maid service in your area.
For just a few dollars they will send someone
to handle the cleanup. Make arrangements for
this in advance and explain that there will be a
party. Also explain exactly what you need the
helper to do.

Thank-You Cards — When to Send Them and What to Write

*O*ver the years I've noticed one common thread with regard to thank-you cards: People like to receive them promptly. It's true that in cases such as a wedding, the happy couple technically has a whole year in which to send thank-you cards. But I **highly recommend** sending them out within a couple of weeks, regardless of the type of event. It can be embarrassing when you run into former guests and have to say, "Oh, we loved your gift, but we haven't gotten around to writing thank-you cards." After all, your guests took the time to RSVP immediately, go out and get an outfit for the party, and purchase a gift. It's only right that you should thank them with the same timely courtesy.

PartyCharlie Tips on Writing Thank-You Notes

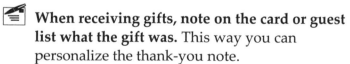

- **When receiving gifts, note on the card or guest list what the gift was.** This way you can personalize the thank-you note.

- **Personalize it.** Write the note yourself rather than send a preprinted thank-you card on which you've simply signed your name.

- **Send a thank-you card for each gift.** In some cases, such as a wedding, you may receive a gift for the shower and then, just a few weeks later, a

wedding gift from the same person. Send a
thank-you card for each gift.

Use "you" more than "I." When writing
thank-you notes, start with "you" as in: "You
were so kind to bring such a lovely gift." Or
"your" as in: "Your gift was such a welcome
surprise." Starting with "I" as in: "I just wanted to
thank you." This keeps the focus on you instead
of the person giving the gift.

Be black and blue. Use traditional colors of ink
(like black and blue) rather than harder-to-read
colors such as red or lavender.

Thank-you's for monetary gifts. Gifts of cash also
require thank-you notes. Money usually comes in
a card, so if you don't want to write, "Thank you
for the money," you can write, "Thank you so
much for the card and the generous gift enclosed
within," or "Thank you so much for the generous
check you sent." If you have plans for the money,
let them know what they are.

Thank-you's for group gifts. If you've received a
group gift given by fewer than 10 people, write a
personal note to each one. If the gift was given by
more than 10 people (co-workers for example),
post a nice note, perhaps on a bulletin board in
the office, and make sure you speak to each
person individually.

What to do if you get a gift you don't like. Write
a simple thank-you note but never ask if you can
exchange the gift.

Section 7

VENDORS and RENTALS

Chapter 43

Vendors — Things to Know and Ask

I know that putting on a party can be a little over-whelming, so don't do everything yourself. Be the captain of your ship — steer it, but bring in the expert "crew" to assist you.

Remember that when you hire vendors and staff, not only are they helping you, but you're helping them by giving them a job. Treat your staff and vendors with respect. Be kind, but let them know what you expect in the way of performance and service.

Working With Vendors Effectively

Below is a list of some of the vendors and service providers you may need:

- Rental companies: Tables and chairs/Linens/ Dishes and glassware/Chafing dishes/Heaters/ Dance floors/Pool covers/tents
- Bakeries
- Balloon suppliers
- Caterers
- Coffee vendors

☐ Decoration companies

☐ Entertainment providers

☐ Florists

☐ Ice suppliers/ice sculptors

☐ Lighting specialists

☐ Music: DJs/Bands/Jukebox suppliers/Karaoke suppliers

☐ Party designers

☐ Party planners

☐ Photographers/Videographers

☐ Security companies

☐ Staffing companies: Bartenders/Wait staff/Cooks/Chefs

☐ Valet parking companies

Making Sure Vendors Are Insured

I can't emphasize enough that any vendors you hire must carry insurance. These are the types of insurance vendors must have:

☐ Workers' compensation

☐ Liability

☐ Auto insurance (if vehicles are entering your property)

Once you know they're insured, here are some tips about vendor insurance:

- [ ] In most cases, just having proof of insurance is fine, but for larger jobs you should be named on the vendor's policy. If that's the case, you may need the vendor to name you as an additionally insured person. This means the insurance policy includes your name for the time the vendor will be on your property.

- [ ] The term of insurance should include the delivery and breakdown days.

- [ ] In the event some vendors work without insurance, such as palm readers or fortune tellers, be aware that if they break or damage something, you may have a hard time recovering the loss if they don't pay to replace or repair it.

- [ ] If you're renting a venue or facility, most likely you will be asked to show that your vendors are insured. Make sure your vendors know that they will have to provide an enforceable insurance policy.

- [ ] Turn the page for one final reminder…

A PartyCharlie Reminder

Which vendors need to be insured when you're hosting a party or event?

EVERY VENDOR NEEDS TO BE INSURED!!!

Working With Your Vendors

☐ Have a budget in mind before you call a vendor. If you don't have any idea of how much you want to or can spend and are calling simply to ask about their charges and services, let them know you're just shopping. Be up-front with them — it's their job to win your trust.

☐ When shopping for vendors, remember to compare apples to apples — be sure you're getting quotes on similar products, services, quantities, and quality.

☐ Don't base your decision solely on price. Also consider the attitude of the vendor, the reputation, the willingness to help with the creative processes and, of course, the service or product itself.

☐ Two days before you plan to pick up or have your products delivered, **call to confirm your order.** If you're using a reputable vendor, your order will likely be fine, but mistakes happen. And in case part or all of your order has been forgotten, a call two days ahead of the event will give the vendor enough time to get the products for you.

☐ When you place your original order for delivery and again when you reconfirm it, be sure to go over the **contents of the order, your address, directions and cross streets, your phone number, and the name of the contact person.**

☐ A note on confirming the address: Include cross streets and directions when you're giving your address to delivery people. In the age of the Internet, when given an address, people have a tendency to say, "I'll just look up the directions myself." This is how Main Street can become Main Avenue in the delivery person's mind, and you end up getting your order a lot later than expected, if at all.

☐ **Confirm the DAY** (for instance, Friday) as well as the **DATE** (June 15th). "The 15th" can sound an awful lot like "the 16th" over the phone. But if you say, "I'm confirming the delivery for Friday the 15th, as in one-five," there won't be any confusion.

☐ Confirm who will meet the deliverer at the party venue, the **time of delivery,** as well as the **day and date.** Make sure they have a copy of your order, and check every item.

The PartyCharlie Vendor Questionnaire

Let's face it, you might not know as much as your professional vendors know about their products or services because they've been doing their job for years. But there are some questions you can ask in order to have a basic understanding of whether or not a particular vendor is right for you. With some help from my PartyCharlie's Vendor Questionnaire, you'll come off like an old pro. I can't tell you how many times I find myself sounding like a complete dummy when I'm talking to someone about software or computers. But party and event vendors I **do** know. And now you will too.

My Vendor Questionnaire can be found in Chapter 55. These are questions you should ask all potential vendors, from caterer, entertainment vendors, photographer, and valet companies to security. This guide will help to ensure that you know what you're getting and that you get what you need.

This vendor questionnaire is so universal, it can be used for anyone you need to hire.

Make sure everything — all special arrangements, requests, vendor attire, tips, etc. — is included in your written contract.

Keeping Track of Vendors You Contact

In Chapter 55, you'll find a handy tool for keeping track of the vendors you call while doing your research – the PartyCharlie Vendor Contact Sheet. It's a lot easier to find details when they're all in one place.

Chapter 44

Rental Company Tips

*H*ere are some general guidelines for using rental companies.

- [ ] Make a list of your requirements before you call a rental company.

- [ ] Go to the rental company's office to see what it has to offer. This is much more effective than just viewing pictures on the Internet.

- [ ] If you go to a rental company and the tables look a little scratched up, fear not — you'll be covering them with tablecloths anyway.

- [ ] Rental companies' services vary. Some provide complete designing service, some will just deliver and set up, and some just deliver and drop off and you do your own setup. Decide what you need.

- [ ] Most rental companies will come to the location where the event is to be held and provide you with a free estimate. Be sure to ask in advance if there is a charge for the estimate. Ask them to show you samples of their products.

- [ ] Some companies provide complete computer-generated layouts drawn to scale, some will sketch the layout by hand, and some will do neither.

- [ ] Get a copy of the confirmed order to review.

☐ **Establish a point person.** This will be the person you'll call with any questions before the delivery of your rentals. And when all goes well, this will be the person you send a thank-you card to for all their hard work.

☐ **A few days before your event, reconfirm your delivery and setup time.** One of the worst scenarios is when the rental company is late on the day of your party.

☐ If possible, have everything delivered the day before the party. Make sure the rentals are set up according to the layout that you or the rental company sketched out. This will minimize the amount of adjusting you'll have to do the day of the event.

☐ When taking delivery of rentals, **check over all the products before you sign for them.** Make sure you receive everything you ordered and that it is in good condition. By signing for the delivery, you take responsibility for the products regardless of the condition they arrived in. And if you're asking someone else to sign for the rentals, **make sure they check over the products, because you're still responsible.**

Tables, Chairs and Umbrellas

☐ Consider all the options. Tables and chairs come in all colors and styles, including white, black, or natural wood or plastic. Some companies also offer chairs that are painted in bright colors and fun designs.

You can cover the tables and chairs in a wide assortment of fabrics to go with the theme of the event.

If your event will be held inside a venue with a high ceiling, umbrellas will appear to bring down the ceiling, making the atmosphere much cozier. If you decorate the insides of the umbrellas with the theme of your party, you'll find that guests will notice and appreciate the added touch.

If your party is outside, tables with umbrellas will keep the sun from burning your guests. Consider renting tables with umbrellas firmly fitted into the center of the table. Umbrellas available from rental companies come in at least two styles: café, which is made of vinyl, and market, which is made of canvas.

Free-standing umbrellas can be set in a movable base, making the umbrellas portable, so you can shade where needed. As the sun moves, so can the umbrellas.

China, Silver, and Glassware for Sit-down Dinners

It's important to know how much china (plateware), silver (flatware), and glassware to rent.

- 🍽 If you're having a sit-down dinner, match your food and beverage items to the plate. Example:
  Entrée = dinner plate, knife, fork, napkin
  Soup = soup bowl or cup, soup spoon
  Dessert = dessert plate, dessert fork

- 🍽 Order a few extra settings in case someone drops a fork.

China, Silver, and Glassware for Buffet-style Service

- 🍽 You'll need 2 dishes per person. Example: 50 people = 100 plates. Most people will use a new plate for seconds.

- 🍽 If the utensils are on the buffet, you should have 2 settings per person as well.

- 🍽 If the utensils are on the table, just have a few extra available.

- 🍽 Provide a separate plate for dessert.

For more information, see Section 3: "Presentation: Putting It All Together."

Chapter 45
Bakeries

Bakery Tips – Working with a Bakery

Consult with the bakery to determine the size of your cake. Take into consideration the number of guests and if the cake will be served in conjunction with lunch, dinner, hors d' oeuvres, or other desserts or will simply be served alone.

Here are some tips for working with a bakery:

- Be sure to give the bakery at least three weeks' notice for special orders.

- If you have a picture of the style of cake or dessert you like, bring it to the bakery.

- Confirm pick-up and/or delivery time.

- If you're picking up the cake, plan ahead for a means of transporting it. Be sure to secure it so it doesn't slide around.

- If the cake is to be delivered, confirm that the bakery has the address, cross street, date and time. For example: Saturday, June 15th, 7:00 p.m.

General Cake-cutting Guidelines

- As long as the cake isn't a surprise and isn't perishable, it's nice to keep it out on display. Place it where it won't get bumped.

- For functions such as an office party, set the cake away from the food and don't place napkins, plates, or the cake-cutting knife near it. This will indicate to guests that the cake will be served later.

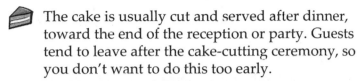 The cake is usually cut and served after dinner, toward the end of the reception or party. Guests tend to leave after the cake-cutting ceremony, so you don't want to do this too early.

Use a sharp knife, especially if your cake has been kept in a freezer or refrigerator.

Keep a tall glass or pitcher of warm water and a towel nearby to dip the knife in before each cut. Wipe the knife clean between slices.

If there is a purpose behind the cake cutting, such as a wedding, play a special song that means something for whom the cake is intended.

You don't need to cut huge pieces. If guests want more, trust me — they will ask!

Cutting Round Cakes

Insert your knife and cut an inner circle. Then make slices 1½–2 inches apart until the entire first ring has been served. Cut the second circle and repeat for the entire layer. Each layer is removed and cut the same way. See the diagram below.

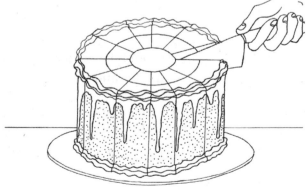

Chapter 46

Caterers

I have enjoyed being a caterer as well as a party planner and party designer for most of my life. Here are tips on my first true love — catering.

If you want the caterer to handle all aspects of the party, go ahead. Use the **PartyCharlie Vendor Questionnaire** to be sure you're getting what you want and need.

Working With a Caterer

1. Get references!

2. Let the caterer assist you in the rental of plateware, utensils, and glassware. First, make up a complete menu. Next, match the rentals to the menu.
   Example: Entrée = dinner plate, knife, fork, napkin.
      Dessert = dessert plate, dessert fork.

3. Insist that the caterer view the venue before you finalize the contract because the venue may already have equipment that the caterer was planning to bring or you had planned to rent. This can save you money.

4. Use my Event Walk-Through Checklist in Chapter 55, PartyCharlie's Templates and Checklists.

5. Ask the caterer to make a diagram showing the placement of the buffet, bar, coffee area, and any other service area. This will ensure the setup runs smoothly.

6. Ask about the quantities of foods to be served, such as how many hors d'oeuvres per person for the cocktail party.

7. Use my portion guide (see Chapter 17, "Food – Preparing Your Own") to be sure you'll have enough food.

8. Ask how many hours the catering staff will continue to serve and replenish food and beverages. The buffet should be left out for a minimum of 1½–2 hours; beverages for the duration of the party.

9. Drinks — yes, the caterer will handle this, but so can you! Provide all the liquor and soft beverages yourself to save $$$$. These can be purchased weeks in advance (see Chapter 29, Bars — Full Service, for information on bars).

10. Order the ice yourself (see Chapter 49, "Keeping Your Party Cool").

11. If you're using disposable ware, get it yourself (see Chapter 23, "Disposable Ware,"). This will save you money, and you can buy it in advance.

12. Hire all the vendors yourself. You have my book as a guide — so save the money. Keep in mind that everything the caterer provides is marked up so they can make a profit.

13. Ask if your caterer will remove the trash from your premises after the party. (See Chapter 35, "Trash – It Stinks, But You Have to Plan for It" for more information on trash.)

Sample Catering Invoice

Make sure the caterer itemizes the invoice for you. A sample invoice can be found in Chapter 55, "PartyCharlie's Templates and Checklists."

Chapter 47

Entertainment

*T*here are many ways to keep your guests entertained. Below are just some of the most popular types of party entertainment. Don't forget to use the **PartyCharlie Vendor Questionnaire** when hiring your entertainment.

List of Entertainment

'50s act
Acrobats and Gymnasts
Artists/Characters
Astrologers
Bagpipers
Balloon Artists
Barbershop Quartet
Big Band
Blues Band
Brass Quintet
Brazilian Dancers
Bubblemakers
Caribbean Dancers
Caricaturists
Celebrity Lookalikes
   and Impersonators
Ceremony Singers
Chamber Ensemble
Classical Guitarist
Classical Pianist
Classical Quartet

Comedians
Costumed Characters
Country & Western Band
Dance Motivators
Dancers
Disc Jockeys (DJ/MC)
Disco Band
Dixieland Band
Doo-Wop Singers
Drag Queens and Female
   Impersonators
Extreme Sports Performers
Face Painters
Fire Eaters
Flamenco Guitarists and
   Dancers
Flute and Guitar Ensemble
Flute and Harp Ensemble
Flute and Piano Ensemble
Flute/Cello/Violin Players
Flute/Guitar/Cello Players

Fortunetellers
Game Coordinators
Handwriting Analysts
Harpist
Henna Artist
Holiday Carolers
Holiday Characters
Hypnotists
Impersonators
International Band
Irish Band
Jugglers
Karaoke Coordinators
Magicians
Mariachi Band
Mimes
One-man Band
Opera Singers

Polynesian Dancers
Psychics
Puppeteers and Puppet
    Shows
Reggae Band
Robots
Salsa/Latin Band
Santa and Elves
Singing Telegrams
Solo Violinists
Steel Drum Band
Stilt Walkers
Strolling Violinists
Top 40 Band
Ventriloquists
Violin and Guitar Players
Wedding Dance Band
Zydeco/Cajun BanD

Interactive Shows and Games

Shows and games are fun and unique performances to add to your event. Vendors can design a show for any situation. Games involve guest participation, whether for the cautiously shy or the outrageously outgoing. If this sounds like fun but services are not available in your area, try contacting a local community or college theater company.

Here are a few suggestions — or, if you're creative, make up your own:

🎭 Murder mystery

🎭 Scavenger hunt

🎭 Game show

🎭 Theatrical
    reenactments

Chapter 48

Florists

Working with Your Florist

❀ If you have a design in mind, that's great, because it will make the florist's job easier and save you time. Bring photos if you have them. However, if you don't know a thing about flowers, don't worry because — guess what — it's the florist's job to guide you through the process.

❀ Once you find something you really like, ask for a sample to be made that you can take with you. If a florist won't give you the flower sample, buy it.

❀ Take the sample to three other florists and begin negotiating. Ask the florist what he or she would charge for the same item.

🎀 If possible, have your flowers delivered or designate someone to pick them up. You can't be everywhere at once, especially if you want to have a little fun at your own party. It's best to have the flowers delivered so your volunteer won't have to wait around while the florist is finishing with other customers. Also, flower delivery vehicles are set up with special racks and shelving in order to transport the flowers safely.

🎀 If you're too busy to get out, or you don't live near any florists, try the Internet. Whether the florist's shop is local or international, the website will have pictures of the kinds of designs they can put together for you.

Choosing Flowers Yourself

🎀 Buy flowers in season to save money. Contact your local florists to find out what flowers are in season or will be in season at the time of your event.

🎀 Fresh flower stems should be green and firm, not dark, discolored, or mushy.

🎀 Using roses that are already open can save you money. Florists don't like to sell roses that are open because customers consider them to be old. However, they certainly have enough life left in them to decorate your buffet for a four-hour party.

🎀 If you want roses that are not already open, check them by gently squeezing the head of the rose. It should feel solid. If a rose feels like a rubber ball, it's ready to bloom and will last only one to two days after it opens.

❀ Flowers that are cut too short for the florist to use, and any flowers that have separated from the stem, will be sold for a fraction of the original cost. They can be effective design touches for your buffet.

❀ Spraying a light mist of Febreze™ over the tops of baby's breath and caspia bundles helps to enhance their aroma.

❀ Be creative! A simple glass vase filled with water and colorful orange or lemon slices with a few flower stems of any kind makes a simple, inexpensive, and beautiful centerpiece. Horsetail in a vase with a few roses is another simple and great looking centerpiece.

❀ Use flowering kale, leather leaves, lemon leaves, and leather ferns to add a beautiful decorative touch to your buffet. For more information on this topic, see Chapter 27, "Buffets – How to Design and Set Them Up Effectively."

Extending the Life of Flowers

❀ You can extend the longevity of most flowers by cutting the stems at a slant under running water as opposed to cutting them in the dry air. Additionally, cutting the stems daily will extend the flowers' life.

❀ To help prevent roses from wilting, submerge them completely in water. While they're under water, shake them until air bubbles come out of the heads. This helps to get the rose to "drink."

✂ Storing cut flowers between 38 and 40 degrees Fahrenheit extends the life of most flowers three to four times.

✂ Tropical flowers should not be exposed to temperatures below 50 degrees.

DO NOT PLACE VASES ON TOP OF TELEVISIONS OR ANY OTHER ELECTRICAL EQUIPMENT!!!

Chapter 49

Keeping Your Party Cool

*S*top running out of ice and stop running out to get more of it. For most people, ice is an afterthought until someone suddenly says, "Hey — we're out of ice." Not to worry — I'll help you keep your party cool with my hot ice tips!

Keeping Your Party on Ice

🍸 If you're planning to have ice delivered from a service, arrange for it to arrive two or three hours before the start of your party. This will give you plenty of time to chill your beverages. Most beverages, when placed in an ice bucket or ice chest, will chill from room temperature to frosty cold in less than an hour. Adding salt accelerates the process.

Y If it's hot and your party is outside, add extra ice to your ice buckets to compensate for faster melting.

Y If your guests are serving themselves, keep a small container with tongs or an ice scoop for your guests to use for ice. You don't want them sticking their hands into a large ice bucket.

Y When icing beverages in buckets or an ice chest, first place the beverages in the bucket. Then add a thin layer of ice and then another layer of beverages. Then completely cover the beverages with ice. You don't have to put ice on the bottom of the bucket or ice chest — the beverages on the bottom are the last to go, and they'll be nice and cold by the time anyone reaches for them. (See diagram below.)

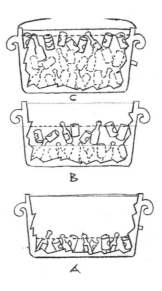

Y I recommend plastic ice chests or tubs. They're less likely to leak and are basically trouble free. Galvanized tubs are also available, but they "sweat" condensation and can cause slippery floors. If you decide to use galvanized tubs, double line them with two large (55-gallon) trash liners, and put a towel under them to absorb the condensation. You don't want Grandma Rose or Big Mike slipping in a puddle.

Y For a nice touch, add a piece of fabric or thick ribbon around the bucket or ice chest. If you have a theme, choose a ribbon that matches the theme.

Y Your washing machine is a great backup for keeping your canned beverages on ice. It has its own drainage system and is ready to go.

Types of Ice

Y Party cube: This is the most common kind of ice used for parties. It's in the shape of — guess what? — a cube.

Y Crushed ice: This is the type of ice you'll order for making blended drinks so you don't have to spend hours running a noisy blender.

Y Block ice: This comes in a large, solid cube. It's hard work to break it up, so I don't recommend it. If left whole, it lasts 50% longer than cube ice.

Ice Quantities

Y On average, for a four-hour party, figure on 2–3 pounds of ice for each guest. If the weather is warm, if you're making frozen drinks and have beverages on ice, or if your guests are active, figure on 3–4 pounds per person.

Y You'll need three to four 20-pound bags of ice for each large cooler or tub.

Y Add a little water to the ice to make the drinks chill more quickly.

Keep It Clean

Don't neglect hygiene when it comes to ice.

Y Line the ice tub with a large plastic trash liner.

Y When you're filling and refilling the ice buckets and chests, pour the cubes from the plastic bags directly into the containers. Don't use your hands.

Y If you have to handle the ice, wear disposable gloves.

Y When icing your drinks, serve the ice with tongs or an ice scoop.

Y If you're chilling bottles and cans on ice, don't use that same ice in the drinks. All the germs on all the hands that ever touched that bottle or can will end up in your drink.

Keep It Safe

Don't use anything breakable, such as a glass, to scoop out ice for your drinks. If the glass cracks without your noticing it, shards and splinters of glass can end up in the drinks.

Thin Ice

When you're transporting food from the restaurant to home, ask the restaurant to give you some ice to pack. Here are some other suggestions:

Fill a plastic zipper freezer bag with about an inch thickness of water. Lay it down in your freezer. When it's frozen, it will be a sheet of ice about the same thickness of ice packs you can purchase at a store. You can make several at once and layer them in the freezer.

Chapter 50

Lighting – Creating Ambiance

I've seen lighting that made the party look like an interrogation room, and I've seen lighting so dim I could barely see.

Sometimes it seems that lighting is the last thing anyone thinks about. But when the lighting reflects a dramatic theme or creates a soothing, fun, or romantic mood, the guests become even more involved. They immediately have a sense of the environment, and it helps them to feel at ease. Utilizing lighting as a way to add ambiance may be a little extra work, but it's worth it. However you handle the lighting, here are some tips on making the most of it.

Lighting for an Indoor Party

Determine what you need weeks in advance. This will save you from last-minute purchases.

Check your lighting a few nights in advance. This will give you the opportunity to make changes and be sure you have the right types of bulbs for your lamps.

Balance your lighting. Avoid creating "hot spots" in the room where too much light causes glare.

Use soft pink or peach-colored bulbs in your lamps. These subtle colors enhance women's makeup, soften everyone's facial lines, and will give your guests an attractive glow.

Party Planning Secrets

○ Use low-wattage bulbs for an intimate mood.

○ Borrow or purchase nice but inexpensive light fixtures and place them on the floor by the end table, behind the sofa, or in a corner by a plant. Bounce the light off the wall for a dramatic effect.

○ If you have a fixture that takes several bulbs, simply unscrew one or two of the bulbs for a dimmer look.

○ If you have track lighting, redirect the lights and cover them with a colored gel to create a colorful splash of light on the wall or highlight a serving area. A color gel is a transparent colored material placed in front of a light fixture. Gels can be purchased through specialty lighting and rental companies.

○ Use lighting to reflect your theme. For instance, you may want to use red lighting for a casino theme, varied colors of bulbs for a circus theme, or spotlights against the walls for a Hollywood theme.

○ Use blacklights for a unique look. No, blacklights are not just a '60s or '70s thing — they can be used for a great effect by placing them around the perimeter of your party area and backing them up against white walls.

○ Place direct lighting on your food area so guests will have a clear view of their choices. But be careful not to overlight the area — food looks best in medium light.

Candles are always great for ambiance, but remember: SAFETY-SAFETY-SAFETY! Oh, and did I mention SAFETY?

If you're using candles to decorate the buffet, place them away from where people will be reaching for the food. Sleeves can get caught in the flame, or the table might get bumped.

If you want to use candles, get hurricane pillar or globe covers to protect the flame.

If you do use candles, make sure you buy the **non-drip type.**

Lighting for an Outdoor Daytime Party

If your party starts during the day and will continue into the evening, be sure to see the next topic for lighting at night.

It's important to know where the shady areas will be during your outdoor party. Once you know the party date and time, walk the venue at the time of the event to see where the shade is. Keep in mind time changes and the angle of the sun as it sets.

During the day, make sure you shade the food, and provide some shade for guests who can't tolerate direct sunlight.

Lighting for an Outdoor Nighttime Party

○ The first thing to do is to walk the property at night with all of your existing lights on. Do this weeks before the party to see what you already have before you begin borrowing, renting, or purchasing lighting equipment.

○ Check a calendar to see which phase the moon will be in on the night of your party — it makes a difference. A few weeks before the party, it might be in a late phase (bright), but by the time of the party, it might be new, producing almost no light — or vice versa.

○ Be sure all entrances, exits, stairs, and steps are well lit.

○ Before the party, check the location of your seating areas and dining tables to make sure that your guests will have enough light to see their food.

○ If you're preparing food outside at night, make sure there's adequate light so you're not burning steaks or fingers in the dark.

○ Even if you're using colored lights for some areas, be sure to provide white light for the food preparation areas so that whoever is cooking can tell when the food is done.

○ Again, if you're using candles, you may want to use hurricane glass to protect the flame.

💡 Be careful when using indoor lamps outdoors. You'll need a sturdy extension cord, and cover it with tape or a rug so people won't trip on it. Make sure you aren't using bulbs that get so hot that they might cause a fire if they're placed near dry items such as leaves, wooden fences, or furniture.

💡 If you need it, borrow additional lighting or purchase some clamp-on spotlights at a hardware or home improvement store. If you need to run extension cords to place the spotlights in strategic areas, make sure you cover them.

💡 Rental companies have several lighting options available. They can set up what's called "pole lighting," also known as "lighting trees." The pole will either be freestanding or will have a spike at the end so it can be "planted" into the ground or tied to a fence or tree. Lighting trees may have two to four lights that can be adjusted in various directions.

💡 Use small or large "par cans," short for "parabolic reflector lamp in a canister." Due to their simplicity and low cost, these are the most popular fixtures for illuminating. Some rental and lighting companies have par cans that put out a large amount of light.

💡 Pin lights throw a beam of light that's great for highlighting items. They're recommended for light beams up to 20 feet. Color lenses are also available from rental or lighting companies.

Party Planning Secrets

An inexpensive option is to break out the old holiday lights — these can create a nice ambiance. I must warn you! Using holiday lights can be labor-intensive, and you'll probably need some extra extension cords.

Chapter 51

Music — DJs, Bands, Jukeboxes, and Karaoke Machines

Music is one of the key components of a party. In all my years in the party business, I've never seen anyone get up and dance because the steak was tender. People will get up and dance if the entertainment raises the energy in the room.

When choosing your music, **know your crowd.** For smaller gatherings, you can probably handle the music yourself. For larger parties, go with a DJ or band. And for something really unique, you might try a jukebox or karaoke machine. Basically, it comes down to doing it yourself or paying someone to handle it for you. Both have their advantages. If you arrange for the music yourself, you'll be saving money. If you hire a DJ or band or rent a jukebox or karaoke machine, you'll be saving time.

Music – Arranging It Yourself

♪ Organizing the music yourself can be a lot of fun, especially if you have the time. However, being tied to the CD player all night doesn't make for a good time. If you want to handle your own music, plan on utilizing your CD changer or borrowing one from a friend. You can also get MP3 players that can hold thousands of songs.

♪ Satellite radio is another option because there are few, if any, commercials.

♪ Choose music from your collection that reflects the theme or tone of the event.

♪ If you borrow CDs, ask if it's alright to place a piece of masking tape on the CD covers and write down the name of the person who lent them to you. Then there won't be any confusion as to whose CDs belong to whom.

♪ If you have a music-loving friend, ask him or her to be your free DJ for the evening. Make sure that you've agreed on the music ahead of time.

♪ If your friend is going play DJ, make sure he or she comes over a day or so before the party to look at the equipment, help to determine the power needs, and figure out the best place to set up.

♪ For a novice DJ, here are some items to have available: a table and linen, extra extension cords and power strips, a small light, and a pad of paper for requests.

Hiring a DJ

Here are some tips for having a trouble-free experience with your DJ.

♫ If you're hiring a caterer or party planner as well as a DJ, make sure they get in touch with one another to coordinate.

♫ Ask the DJ to visit the party venue to scout it out.

♫ DJs love to work where everyone can see them. Putting the DJ in an accessible place also allows your guests to make requests.

♫ The DJ can also act as the master of ceremonies (MC) to keep people informed and involved.

♫ If you don't want your DJ to be the main focus or act as the MC, place him/her in a discreet corner. Make sure you let your DJ know that all you want is good music.

♫ Find out if the DJ provides party favors for the guests. Often, the DJ will give away novelties, such as lighted bracelets, neon balloons, or small inflatable guitars.

♫ DJ's can also provide dancers to get your guests involved.

♫ Specify the songs that are important to you. If you absolutely must have certain songs, make sure this is written into your contract. If you just mention your preferences in casual conversation, the DJ might not realize how important they are to you.

♪ Ask the DJ to provide you with a list of songs in his/her inventory.

♪ Before deciding whether you want a particular DJ, arrange to go see his/her setup.

♪ Ask your DJ if he/she needs a table for equipment setup. If a table is needed, be sure to provide a drape or cloth.

♪ DJs' rates can vary. I recommend calling three of them in your area for quotes. Fees vary depending on the DJ's experience, how long you want him/her to play, and the equipment he/she is providing.

♪ GET EVERYTHING IN WRITING. The contract should contain everything you and the DJ agreed upon.

Tips for Using a Band

Finding a band involves a process similar to finding a DJ. Here are some tips to make it easier.

♪ Most bands will provide a demo CD or videotape.

♪ Once you've heard or seen the demo tape, go see them live, if possible.

♪ Band rates vary. I recommend calling about three of them in your area for quotes. Fees vary depending on the band's experience, how long you want them to play, how many musicians are in the band, and the equipment they're providing.

♫ Don't pick a 10-piece band if the area you've planned for them will be cramped. Consult the band regarding the space they will need.

♫ If the party is too loud, people will have a hard time holding conversations, and you'll be risking a visit from the neighbors — or worse, the police. Talk to your neighbors in advance to let them know you'll be having a party and when the band will stop playing.

♫ Don't be afraid to tell the band to lower the volume. Remember, this is your party.

♫ GET EVERYTHING IN WRITING. The contract should contain everything you and the band agreed upon.

Tips for Using Jukeboxes

♫ Jukeboxes are especially fun for nostalgia parties. They can be set up to play without money.

♫ You may be able to rent jukeboxes in your area at party supply companies, or look under "Juke Box Services" in the phone book or on the Internet. Companies that sell and service jukeboxes may also be willing to rent them.

♫ If you can't find jukebox providers, ask your local party supply or rental company for references or leads.

♫ Make sure you have enough power to handle a jukebox.

♪ Have a safe place to put the jukebox so you're in compliance with the rental guidelines.

♪ Make sure that the people delivering the jukebox will also be setting it up, ensuring that it works properly, and giving you all the instructions for operating it before they leave.

Tips for Using a Karaoke Machine

♪ Like a jukebox, karaoke can be a fun addition to the party, although you really must know your crowd and whether or not they will be willing to participate.

♪ You can hire a service, rent, or even buy a karaoke machine.

♪ You can find karaoke services in the phonebook or on the Internet, or by calling party supply and rental companies.

♪ Make sure your karaoke machine is set up where all your guests can see it.

♪ You must have a charismatic karaoke MC who has a great singing voice and can keep the music going even when your guests aren't ready to sing.

♪ Ask the vendor to provide you with a karaoke sign-up sheet and a song list.

♪ Make it fun with a panel of judges, and give prizes to the best singers.

♪ Always keep your power needs in mind, and ask the vendor what the machine requires.

Chapter 52

Pictures — Photographers and Videographers

Sometimes choosing a photographer or videographer can be a stressful experience. After all, photos and videos are the tangible memories of your gathering. So here are some basic tips on making the right choice.

Tips for Your Photographer/Videographer

📷 Make sure you're getting who you think you're getting. Many photography and videography studios utilize subcontractors. So the friendly, experienced guy or gal you speak with on the phone or even meet in person might not be the same one who shows up to take your pictures or record the video on the day of your event. Insist on meeting the person who will be working that day. He or she might be very talented, but you want to feel comfortable with whoever is there on your special day.

📷 Ask if they will be using VHS, DVD, or mini-DV.

📷 Look at samples. Whether you're choosing a photographer or videographer or both, this is the best way to determine whether the quality and style matches what you're looking for.

📷 Choose a style that works for you. Research various styles that are available and choose someone who specializes in that style.

📷 Give the photographer/videographer a printout of pictures of the VIPs or family members complete with names and VIP status/relationship to you. This way they are sure to take lots of photos of the people most important to you.

📷 Don't skimp. I know this is a book on how to save money, but trust me — even if pictures don't seem like a big priority, when you look back on your party or event, you'll want something nice by which to remember it. You may be able to have pictures or videos done inexpensively, but make sure they won't look cheap.

📷 Inexpensive and cheap are two different things. One way to save money if you live in a metropolitan area is by choosing someone outside the city. Generally, those photographers are less expensive, but can be just as highly skilled.

Special Questions to Ask Your Photographer or Videographer

1. Will you be taking the pictures/videotaping personally, or will someone else do it?

2. Can you come before the event to shoot/videotape the setting-up process?

3. How many exposures/how many hours of tape do you take?

4. When will the proofs/edited video be ready?

5. Can I see a portfolio/edited video from one of your recent events?

6. Can I see a proof book/unedited video from one of your recent events?

7. How long will it take to receive prints/video copies once they are ordered?

8. Are the negatives and/or unedited video available to purchase, and if so, do I have to wait a specified time before I can purchase them?

9. For pictures: Do you shoot in film or digital?
   For video: Do you shoot in VHS or digital?

10. Do you shoot in black and white, color, or both? (This can apply to both photographs and videos.)

11. What is the time frame when I can order additional prints/videos at the quoted price?

12. How much do you charge? What types of packages do you offer? What is your payment plan? What are the overtime charges?

13. Are discounts available if I want to purchase duplicates?

Chapter 53

Security — Protecting You, Your Family, and Your Guests

Security professionals are trained to deal with emergencies, and they help you and your guests feel safe. To determine if your event requires security, listed below are some questions to ask yourself.

1. Will there be valuable property or large sums of money present?

2. Will there be guests who might draw media attention?

3. Do I have enough trained volunteers or staff people?

4. Is admission paid or free?

5. Is the event open to the public, as in a charity event, or open only to guests?

6. Will the event be advertised?

7. Will there be other events going on in nearby venues (such as more than one wedding at a country club)?

Some Rules of Basic Security

☐ Whether the party is indoors, outdoors, or in a private venue or public one, have a guest list at the entrance. As people arrive, check their names off the list (or have a volunteer do it). This may sound formal, but it's better to be safe than to have uninvited guests at your party.

☐ A guest list is only as private as you allow it to be. Don't permit would-be party crashers to view the guest list — that gives them the opportunity to pick a random name to use.

☐ Decorative wristbands, themed T-shirts or hats, or nametags can distinguish guests from party-crashers, particularly if the party is in a public area, such as a park.

☐ If you do want security professionals at your party, arrange for it at least 30 days in advance.

Chapter 54

Valet Parking and Shuttle Service — The Comings and Goings

Determining How Many Valet Service Attendants You'll Need

Here's how to calculate the cost and number of valet attendants you'll need:

- Generally, you'll need one parking attendant per 12 cars. If the parking area is far from the entrance to your party, you may need additional attendants. Check with the valet company; it may be necessary for the vendor to survey your area.

- You'll need one valet to stay where your guests' car keys are placed (called the "key box").

Hiring a Valet Service

- Ask about hiring practices. Find out if the company confirms driver's licenses before hiring and if it does spot checks of driving records.

- Check with local businesses, such as managers at local clubs and hotels, and ask whom they would recommend.

Party Planning Secrets

🚗 Parking attendants should provide the following: flashlights, reflective cones, signs to let people know valet service is available, a key box, uniforms, and valet tickets.

🚗 When you're providing valet service, post signs reading "Valet parking service for Smith party."

🚗 If you don't want your guests to tip, you must include a gratuity. If you **are** including the gratuities, ask if the valet company provides a sign saying "Gratuities Provided by Host" so guests don't feel obligated to tip.

🚗 Ask your valet company to check with City Hall to find out if you need any licenses or permits.

🚗 Inform your neighbors. They will appreciate your notifying them before allowing guests to park in front of their homes.

🚗 Plan for limited parking. One way to save time and expense is by hiring a valet strictly to run a shuttle service to and from a predesignated parking area and your party.

🚗 If the area where the cars are parked is far from the party, the valet should have some way to easily communicate, such as via walkie talkies. If the valet company makes them available, find out if you'll incur any charge for them.

🚗 Prepare for the weather. Make sure the valet service has umbrellas for rain, as well as snow removal equipment (such as ice scrapers, salt,

sand, and snow shovels) during the winter months.

🚗 Have the valet service visit the property before the party so it can verify the parking lots, locations, and local rules. Also discuss security concerns.

🚗 Ask if the company takes care of its staff, such as providing meals. If it doesn't, expect to provide this yourself.

🚗 Ensure that the company has a written "no alcohol" policy.

🚗 Get more bang for your buck: If you'll be providing special thank-you gifts for all your guests, have the valet staff give one to each guest as he/she leaves the party. (Set up the gift table after everyone has arrived but early enough to accommodate guests who will be leaving the party early.)

Chapter 55

PartyCharlie's Templates and Checklists

*W*ell, folks, you've come to the valuable resources of this book — templates and checklists that will help you plan and carry out outrageously exciting and successful parties. They're designed to help you organize all the many details of your party so you can worry less and enjoy yourself more.

Here's what you'll find in this chapter:

- PartyCharlie Budget Worksheet
- PartyCharlie Party Checklist
- PartyCharlie 1-2-3 Buffet Setup
- PartyCharlie Event Walk-Through Checklist
- PartyCharlie Vendor Questionnaire
- PartyCharlie Vendor Contact Sheet
- Sample Catering Invoice
- PartyCharlie First Aid Kit Supply Checklist
- PartyCharlie Safety Checklist

Rather than write in the book, feel free to make as many copies of these forms as you need or go to my website, www.PartyCharlie.com, click on Party Planning Secrets, then click on Templates and Checklists. You'll have them to use for all your future parties.

PartyCharlie Budget Worksheet

Event Type	Date	Time	Number of Guests	Location
	Budgeted Amount	**Actual Cost**	**Deposit Paid**	**Amount Due**
Event Location – Venue				
Power	$	$	$	$
Water – 5-gallon container	$	$	$	$
Rental fee for venue	$	$	$	$
Insurance	$	$	$	$
Tenting	$	$	$	$
Heaters	$	$	$	$
Lighting	$	$	$	$
Scenery, props, other decor	$	$	$	$
Flowers	$	$	$	$
Special permits	$	$	$	$
Subtotal	**$**	**$**	**$**	**$**
Staff				
Event planner	$	$	$	$
Chef	$	$	$	$
Cook	$	$	$	$
Wait staff	$	$	$	$
Bartender	$	$	$	$
Hostesses	$	$	$	$
Errand person	$	$	$	$
Clean-up help	$	$	$	$
Miscellaneous	$	$	$	$
Subtotal	$	$	$	$

Continued

264

Party Planning Secrets

Event Type	Date	Time	Number of Guests	Location
	Budgeted Amount	**Actual Cost**	**Deposit Paid**	**Amount Due**
Food & Beverages				
Appetizers	$	$	$	$
Entrees	$	$	$	$
Desserts	$	$	$	$
Wine	$	$	$	$
Liquor	$	$	$	$
Beer	$	$	$	$
Garnishes (limes, olives, etc.)	$	$	$	$
Soft beverages/juices	$	$	$	$
Ice	$	$	$	$
Coffee	$	$	$	$
Subtotal	**$**	**$**	**$**	**$**
Invitations				
Design	$	$	$	$
Printing	$	$	$	$
Addressing	$	$	$	$
Postage	$	$	$	$
Save-the-date cards	$	$	$	$
Thank-you cards	$	$	$	$
Subtotal	**$**	**$**	**$**	**$**
Disposable Ware				
Tablecloths - plastic or paper	$	$	$	$
Napkins - food and cocktail	$	$	$	$
Plates - dinner and dessert	$	$	$	$
Cups - coffee	$	$	$	$

Continued

Event Type	Date	Time	Number of Guests	Location
	Budgeted Amount	Actual Cost	Deposit Paid	Amount Due
Disposable Ware (Continued)				
Tumblers	$	$	$	$
Utensils	$	$	$	$
Straws, stirrers, & toothpicks for bar drinks	$	$	$	$
Trash liners	$	$	$	$
Subtotal	**$**	**$**	**$**	**$**
Rentals				
Tables	$	$	$	$
Chairs	$	$	$	$
Dishes	$	$	$	$
Glassware	$	$	$	$
Silverware	$	$	$	$
Serving dishes	$	$	$	$
Linens	$	$	$	$
Buffet table	$	$	$	$
Portable bar	$	$	$	$
Dance floor	$	$	$	$
Lighting safety	$	$	$	$
Lighting/Ambiance	$	$	$	$
Miscellaneous	$	$	$	$
Subtotal	**$**	**$**	**$**	**$**

Continued

Party Planning Secrets

Event Type	Date	Time	Number of Guests	Location
	Budgeted Amount	Actual Cost	Deposit Paid	Amount Due
Entertainment				
Musicians	$	$	$	$
Entertainers	$	$	$	$
Disc jockey	$	$	$	$
Sound system	$	$	$	$
Spotlights	$	$	$	$
Subtotal	$	$	$	$
Accessories				
Nametags	$	$	$	$
Place cards	$	$	$	$
Bathroom towels/accessories	$	$	$	$
Ashtrays	$	$	$	$
Matches	$	$	$	$
Party favors	$	$	$	$
Gift bags	$	$	$	$
Miscellaneous	$	$	$	$
Subtotal	$	$	$	$
Services				
Photographer	$	$	$	$
Videographer	$	$	$	$
Valet service	$	$	$	$
Electrician	$	$	$	$
Security personnel	$	$	$	$
Coat check attendant	$	$	$	$
Subtotal	$	$	$	$

Continued

Event Type	Date	Time	Number of Guests	Location
	Budgeted Amount	Actual Cost	Deposit Paid	Amount Due
Transportation				
Chartered buses	$	$	$	$
Limousines	$	$	$	$
Taxi cabs	$	$	$	$
Refreshments for trip	$	$	$	$
Driver tips/gratuities	$	$	$	$
Miscellaneous	$	$	$	$
Subtotal	$	$	$	$
Miscellaneous				
Service charges	$	$	$	$
Gratuities	$	$	$	$
Miscellaneous	$	$	$	$
Subtotal	$	$	$	$
Totals				
Combined subtotals	$	$	$	$
Total sales tax	$	$	$	$
Contingency allowance (about 5%)	$	$	$	$
TOTAL EXPENSES	$	$	$	$

PartyCharlie Party Checklist

6–8 WEEKS BEFORE
Budget:
Theme:
Type of party (formal, casual):
Location:
Number of guests (create list):
Type of menu (buffet, potluck, family style):
Start time:
Finish time:
Buy/design invitations:

3–4 WEEKS BEFORE
Mail invitations:
Plan menu:
Shopping list:
Decide what you're putting the food in:
Where you're placing the platters:
Plan buffets:
Plan utensils (eating and serving):
Start looking for disposable ware sales:
Plan on china, silver, glassware rentals:
Plan on table/chair rentals:
Extra chairs to accommodate guests:
Linens (buy, borrow, rent):
PartyCharlie 1-2-3 Buffet Set Up:
Seating arrangements:
Plan on decorations:
Design flower arrangements:
Hire valet service:
Hire coat check:
Hire photographer:
Entertainment (DJ, band, games, speeches):
Plan food schedule (what time to start/finish serving appetizers, entrée, dessert):

Continued

3–4 WEEKS BEFORE (Continued)
Coffee/tea:
Dessert:
Appetizers/hors d'oeuvres:
Entrée:
Dessert/coffee:
Plan on scullery (cleanup and trash) area:
Plan bar (self-service, full service):
Plan beverages:
Arrange for bartender:
Servers:
Hire caterer:
Valet parking:
Decide on what time should staff arrive/leave:
Choose staff attire:
Ensure adequate power supply/water:
Make list of areas where you could use volunteers:
Accept help:
1–2 WEEKS BEFORE
Buy disposable ware/order rentals:
Purchase beverages:
Buy nonperishable foods:
Confirm number of guests:
Designate smoking area:
Buy decorations:
Buy party favors:
Outline the flow of the party:
2–3 DAYS BEFORE
Confirm rental arrivals/pickup:
Clean house/yard:
Arrange supplies for party:
Put away breakable items:
Make a polite call to potential guests who haven't RSVP'd:
Have lighting equipment set up and tested (if indoors):

Continued

Party Planning Secrets

1 DAY BEFORE
Prearrange any foods that can be stored in refrigerator/freezer:
Complete food preparation and pickup of pre-ordered food items:
Do indoor decorating for the party:
Set tables/serving tables (lay out all disposable and glassware):
Place Post-It notes on bowls, buffet tables, counter spaces indicating what will go there:

DAY OF PARTY
Staff arrives:
Set table/buffet:
Decorate/floral:
Prepare any foods that couldn't be prepared in advance:
Set up scullery/trash areas:
Do outdoor decorating/table setup:
Have ice delivered:
Have lighting equipment set up and tested (if outdoors):
Ensure entertainment area is set up:
Have Fun!!!

PartyCharlie 1-2-3 Buffet Setup

MENU ITEMS	SERVING EQUIPMENT NEEDED	ADDED TO DIAGRAM

PartyCharlie Event Walk-Through Checklist

Client Name: _____

Phone #:_____Cell # _____

Secondary Contact: _____

Phone #:_____Cell # _____

Event Location:_____

Other:_____

E-mail:_____

Event Date: _____

Time Start: _____ Event End Time: _____

Number of Guests: _____

Delivery time: _____

ACCESS TO PARTY LOCATION FOR TRUCKS & EQUIPMENT

Access on to Property:_____

Time:_____ Contact name:_____

Contact number_____

Drive Way:_____

Side Entrance:_____

Restrictions for Vehicle unloading:_____

_____

Low building / Access:_____

Other:_____

STAFF PARKING

Fee for Staff Parking:_____Paid By:_____

TRASH AREA

Indoor Trash Area:_____

Outdoor Trash Area:_____

Trash Pickup Days:_____

Number of Trash Cans:_____

Other:_____

_____

Continued

CLIENT'S KITCHEN

Stove top – Number of Burners: _____

Number of Ovens:_____ Oven Size(s): _____

Microwave:_____ Refrigeration: _____ Freezer:_____

Kitchen Size:_____

Counter top:_____Sinks:_____

Power – Number of Outlets:_____

Other:_____

CLIENT'S GARAGE

Size:_____Entrances:_____Lights:_____

Sink:_____Power: _____ Refrigeration:_____

Other:_____

PARTY RECEPTION AREA INDOORS

Size:_____

Power:_____

Lighting:_____

Scullery*:_____

*Scullery: A place designated to place used dishes, etc.

PARTY RECEPTION AREA OUTDOORS

Sun Related to Buffet/Bar/Guest:_____

Bar:_____

Buffet:_____

Scullery:_____

Sprinklers:_____

SPECIAL REQUEST

Registration Table:_____

Gift Table:_____

PA System:_____

Guest Seating Arrangements:_____

Entertainment:_____

PartyCharlie Vendor Questionnaire

Vendor Name: _____

Address: _____

_____

Phone (Work): _____

Phone (Home): _____

Phone (Cell): _____

E-mail: _____

General

How many parties/events/jobs do you do in a year?

_____

Do you have references from the last three parties/events/jobs you've done?

_____

Do you have proof of insurance?

_____

(Ask for a current copy. It is **very important** to obtain a current copy of the insurance policy.)

Are you a member of the Chamber of Commerce/BBB?

_____

Who will be the contact person I can easily reach to ask questions?

_____

Will that person be available via cell phone, and during what hours?

_____

Who can I reach after hours or in case of an emergency?

_____

Costs

What are your rates?

_____

Is there an overtime charge?

_____

When does this occur? (Example: after 8 hours?)

_____

(Overtime should be negotiated before signing the contract. Get it in writing.)

Continued

Toward the end of your party, if you feel overtime is needed, then by all means let the vendor know.)

What hours are you open/available?

How long will it take you to set up?

Are there any additional charges not already mentioned?

(Example: travel costs)

What items on the bill are taxable?

Is a gratuity or service charge included in the price?_____
If not, is there a flat rate for the gratuity or service charge?

How many consultations do you provide in your package price?

What are the refund and cancellation terms?

Are these listed in the contract?

Is a deposit required? If so, how much?

When is the final payment due?

What forms of payment do you accept?

(Examples: credit cards, personal check)

<u>Miscellaneous</u>

Do you provide a written contract?

Do you need a guarantee on the number of guests? _____
If so, when do you need the final guest count?

Continued

Party Planning Secrets

What does your setup look like?

_____

What do your buffet and service areas consist of?

_____

Do you have pictures?

_____

What are your space requirements?

_____

What are your power requirements?

_____

What type of equipment do you use?

_____

Do you have a backup plan and backup equipment?

_____

Will you visit the event site beforehand to determine any special needs?

_____

Can I provide a list of "must haves"?

_____
(Examples: songs, photos, types of food, types of flowers)

What restrictions do you have in your service?

_____
(Example: What can't or won't you do?)

What is your and your staff's standard attire?

_____

If this is a special occasion or theme party, will you dress according to the event if necessary?

_____

Do you have a zero drinking and drug tolerance policy for your staff?

_____

Do you provide meals for yourself/your staff?

_____
(You may be required to feed your vendors. Always discuss this in advance. If you're hiring a caterer, he/she may discount other vendors' meals, such as the entertainment.)

PartyCharlie Vendor Contact Sheet

BAKERIES

Contact 1   Name: _____

Address: _____

E-mail: _____

Phone: _____

Circle: Inexpensive   Moderate   Expensive

Did I feel comfortable with this person? ___

Contact 2   Name: _____

Address: _____

E-mail: _____

Phone: _____

Circle: Inexpensive   Moderate   Expensive

Did I feel comfortable with this person? ___

BARTENDERS

Contact 1   Name: _____

Address: _____

E-mail: _____

Phone: _____

Circle: Inexpensive   Moderate   Expensive

Did I feel comfortable with this person? ___

Contact 2   Name: _____

Address: _____

E-mail: _____

Phone: _____

Circle: Inexpensive   Moderate   Expensive

Did I feel comfortable with this person? ___

Continued

<u>**CATERERS**</u>

Contact 1 Name: _____

Address: _____

E-mail: _____

Phone: _____

Circle: Inexpensive   Moderate   Expensive

Did I feel comfortable with this person? ___

Contact 2 Name: _____

Address: _____

E-mail: _____

Phone: _____

Circle: Inexpensive   Moderate   Expensive

Did I feel comfortable with this person? ___

<u>**COAT CHECK SERVICES**</u>

Contact 1 Name: _____

Address: _____

E-mail: _____

Phone: _____

Circle: Inexpensive   Moderate   Expensive

Did I feel comfortable with this person? ___

Contact 2 Name: _____

Address: _____

E-mail: _____

Phone: _____

Circle: Inexpensive   Moderate   Expensive

Did I feel comfortable with this person? ___

Continued

ELECTRICIANS/LIGHTING

Contact 1   Name: _____

Address: _____

E-mail: _____

Phone: _____

Circle: Inexpensive   Moderate   Expensive

Did I feel comfortable with this person? ___

Contact 2   Name: _____

Address: _____

E-mail: _____

Phone: _____

Circle: Inexpensive   Moderate   Expensive

Did I feel comfortable with this person? ___

ENTERTAINMENT PROVIDERS

Contact 1   Name: _____

Address: _____

E-mail: _____

Phone: _____

Circle: Inexpensive   Moderate   Expensive

Did I feel comfortable with this person? ___

Contact 2   Name: _____

Address: _____

E-mail: _____

Phone: _____

Circle: Inexpensive   Moderate   Expensive

Did I feel comfortable with this person? ___

Continued

FLORISTS

Contact 1 Name: _____

Address: _____

E-mail: _____

Phone: _____

Circle: Inexpensive   Moderate   Expensive

      Did I feel comfortable with this person? ___

Contact 2 Name: _____

Address: _____

E-mail: _____

Phone: _____

Circle: Inexpensive   Moderate   Expensive

      Did I feel comfortable with this person? ___

ICE SUPPLIERS

Contact 1 Name: _____

Address: _____

E-mail: _____

Phone: _____

Circle: Inexpensive   Moderate   Expensive

      Did I feel comfortable with this person? ___

Contact 2 Name: _____

Address: _____

E-mail: _____

Phone: _____

Circle: Inexpensive   Moderate   Expensive

      Did I feel comfortable with this person? ___

Continued

PARTY PLANNERS

Contact 1 Name: _____
Address: _____
E-mail: _____
Phone: _____
Circle: Inexpensive Moderate Expensive

Did I feel comfortable with this person? ___

Contact 2 Name: _____
Address: _____
E-mail: _____
Phone: _____
Circle: Inexpensive Moderate Expensive

Did I feel comfortable with this person? ___

PHOTOGRAPHERS

Contact 1 Name: _____
Address: _____
E-mail: _____
Phone: _____
Circle: Inexpensive Moderate Expensive

Did I feel comfortable with this person? ___

Contact 2 Name: _____
Address: _____
E-mail: _____
Phone: _____
Circle: Inexpensive Moderate Expensive

Did I feel comfortable with this person? ___

Continued

RENTAL SERVICES

Contact 1 Name: _____

Address: _____

E-mail: _____

Phone: _____

Circle: Inexpensive   Moderate   Expensive

Did I feel comfortable with this person? ___

Contact 2 Name: _____

Address: _____

E-mail: _____

Phone: _____

Circle: Inexpensive   Moderate   Expensive

Did I feel comfortable with this person? ___

SECURITY SERVICES

Contact 1 Name: _____

Address: _____

E-mail: _____

Phone: _____

Circle: Inexpensive   Moderate   Expensive

Did I feel comfortable with this person? ___

Contact 2 Name: _____

Address: _____

E-mail: _____

Phone: _____

Circle: Inexpensive   Moderate   Expensive

Did I feel comfortable with this person? ___

Continued

VALET SERVICES

Contact 1 Name: _____
Address: _____
E-mail: _____
Phone: _____
Circle: Inexpensive Moderate Expensive

      Did I feel comfortable with this person? ___

Contact 2 Name: _____
Address: _____
E-mail: _____
Phone: _____
Circle: Inexpensive Moderate Expensive

      Did I feel comfortable with this person? ___

WAIT STAFF

Contact 1 Name: _____
Address: _____
E-mail: _____
Phone: _____
Circle: Inexpensive Moderate Expensive

      Did I feel comfortable with this person? ___

Contact 2 Name: _____
Address: _____
E-mail: _____
Phone: _____
Circle: Inexpensive Moderate Expensive

      Did I feel comfortable with this person? ___

Sample Catering Invoice

Social Catering by Charlie Scola aka PartyCharlie
Charlie's direct Line 310-555-XXXX: Charliescola@earthlink.net   www.PartyCharlie.com   **Date of Event:** January 5, 20XX **Invoice #:** 10356   **Name:** Rosemarie Ray   **Address:** Mender Rd.   **City:** Seaside   **State** XX **Zip** XXXXX   **Phone:** 310-555-XXXX

Description Of Service Or Product Provided	Quantity	Unit Price	Total
Passed Hors d'oeuvres	100	$ 12.00	$1200.00
Main Meal	100	$ 31.00	$3100.00
Dessert	100	$ 6.00	$ 600.00
Coffee	100	$ 3.50	$ 350.00
Beverage – nonalcoholic	100	$ 4.00	$ 400.00
Ice – 40 lb. bags	8 bags	$ 10.00	$ 80.00
Water	1-5 Gal.	$ 9.00	$ 9.00
*All staff based on eight hours; overtime after 8 hours at time and half rate			
*Party Manager	1	$350.00	$ 350.00
*Chef	1	$350.00	$ 350.00
*Kitchen Staff	1	$300.00	$ 300.00
*Server	4	$200.00	$ 800.00
*Bartender	1	$200.00	$ 200.00
Rental, Flowers, Entertainment not included in price			

PAYMENT DETAILS		
APPROVED BY: _____	Subtotal	$7739.00
CHECK #: _____	Service Charge 18%	$1393.02
DATE CHECK CUT: _____	Tax 8.25%	$ 753.39
DATE CHECK SENT: _____	Total	$9885.41

Please visit our website at www.PartyCharlie.com
Thank you for your business

PartyCharlie First Aid Kit Supply Checklist

First Aid Kit Supply Checklist			
First Aid Kit Supplies	**On Hand**	**Acquire**	**Accomplished**
Antiseptic wipes			
Aspirin tablets			
Elastic adhesive strips			
Elastic fingertip bandages			
Elastic patch bandages			
Finger splint			
First aid tape			
Gauze bandage			
Hand sanitizer			
Hydrocortisone cream			
Ibuprofen tablets			
Large bone splint			
Latex exam gloves			
Medical shears			
Nonaspirin tablets			
Pain-relieving burn ointment			
Porous cloth adhesive tape			
Sterile dressing			
Sterile eye pads			
Triple antibiotic ointment			

PartyCharlie Safety Checklist

PARTYCHARLIE SAFETY CHECKLIST	On Hand	Acquire	Accomplished
Lights are positioned safely.			
Light fixtures are secure.			
Cords are tucked away so guests won't trip over them.			
Entrances and exits are well lit.			
Fire extinguisher is on hand.			
Emergency numbers are posted next to the phone.			
Lifeguard on hand for swimming pool.			
Security personnel on hand if the party is in an open area.			
Bar supervisor to check that no underage drinkers are being served.			
Unbreakable (plastic or metal) scoop for scooping out ice.			
Sink guard placed over the garbage disposal.			
Knife block or area set aside specifically for the cutting knives.			
Mop and bucket handy in case of spills, and a broom and dustpan for dry spills or any breakage that happens.			
First aid instructions reviewed.			
Location of first aid kits discussed with servers or volunteers.			
Flashlight in working order.			

Appendix

Cloth Napkin
Folding Instructions

PYRAMID

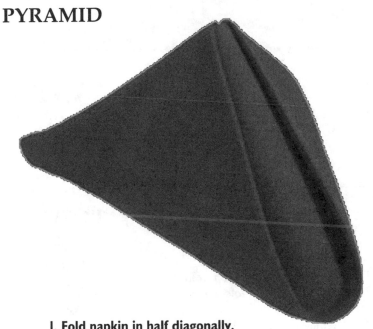

1. **Fold napkin in half diagonally.**
2. **Fold corners to meet top point.**
3. **Turn napkin over and fold in half.**
4. **Pick up at center and stand on base of triangle.**

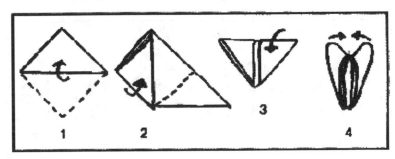

THE ROSE

1. Fold all 4 corners of open napkin to center.
2. Fold new corners to center.
3. Turn napkin over and fold all corners to center.
4. Holding center firmly, reach each corner and pull up to form petals. Reach petals and pull flaps underneath.

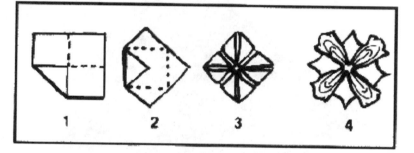

1   2   3   4

ROSEBUD

1. Fold napkin in half diagonally.
2. Fold corners to meet at top point.
3. Turn napkin over and fold bottom 2/3 way up.
4. Turn napkin around and bring corners together, tucking one into the other.
5. Turn napkin around and stand on base.

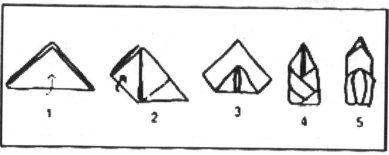

1   2   3   4   5

ARUM LILY

1. Fold napkin bringing bottom up to top.
2. Fold corners to top.
3. Fold bottom point up to 1" below top.
4. Fold point back onto itself.
5. Fold down each of points at top and tuck under edge of folded-up bottom. Fold down one layer of top point and tuck under base fold.
6. Turn napkin over and tuck left and right sides into each other.
7. Open base and stand.

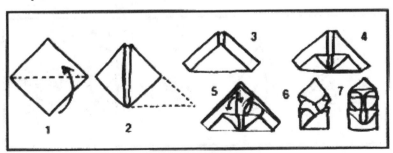

THE CROWN

1. Fold napkin in half diagonally.
2. Fold corners to meet at top point.
3. Fold bottom point 2/3 way to top and fold back onto itself.
4. Turn napkin over bringing together, tucking one into the other.
5. Peel two top corners to make crown.
6. Open base of fold and stand upright.

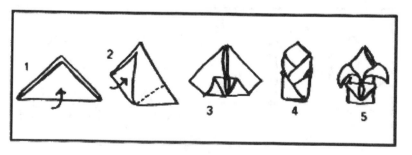

CARDINAL'S HAT

1. Fold napkin in half diagonally.
2. Fold corners to meet at top point.
3. Turn napkin over with points to the top, fold lower corner 2/3 way up.
4. Fold back onto itself.
5. Bring corners together tucking one into the other.
6. Open base of fold and stand upright.

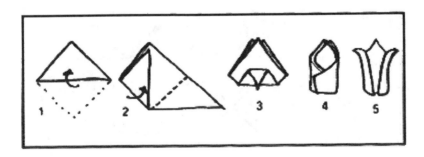

BISHOP'S MITRE

1. Fold napkin bringing top to bottom.
2. Fold corners to center line.
3. Turn napkin over and rotate ¼ turn.
4. Fold bottom edge up to top edge and flip point out from under top fold.
5. Turn left end into pleat at left forming a point on left side.
6. Turn napkin over and turn right end into pleat forming a point on right side.
7. Open base and stand upright.

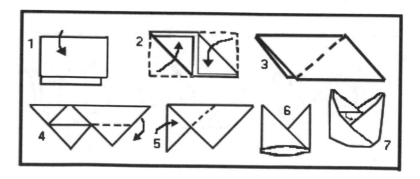

CLOWN'S HAT

1. Fold napkin in half bringing bottom to top.
2. Holding center of bottom with finger, take lower right corner and loosely roll around center, matching corners, until cone is formed.
3. Turn napkin upside down, then turn hem all around.
4. Turn and stand on base.

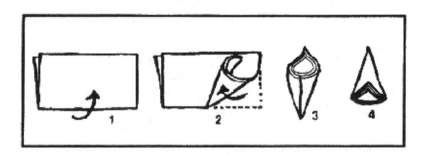

BIRD OF PARADISE

1. Fold napkin in half, and then half again horizontally.
2. Then fold in half diagonally with points on the top and facing up.
3. Fold left and right sides down along center line, turning their extended points under.
4. Fold points of bottom corners underneath and fold in half on long end.
5. Pull up points and arrange fabric on a surface.

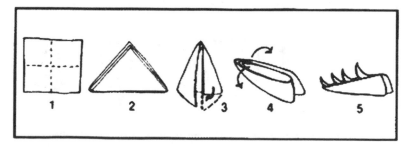

298

LADY WINDERMERE'S FAN

1. Fold napkin in half.
2. Make half with pleats.
3. Fold in half with pleating on the outside.
4. Fold upper right corner diagonally down to folded base of pleats and turn under edge.
5. Place on table and release pleats to form fan.

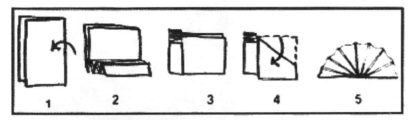

GOBLET FAN

1. Fold napkin in half.
2. Pleat from bottom to top.
3. Turn napkin back 1/3 of the way on right (folded) end and place into goblet.
4. Spread out pleats at top.

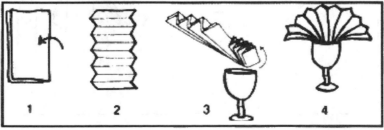

THE CANDLE

1. Fold napkin in half diagonally.
2. Fold down base 1/3 of the way.
3. Turn napkin over and roll from bottom to top.
4. Tuck corners inside cuff at base of fold and stand.
5. Turn one layer of point down and set on base.

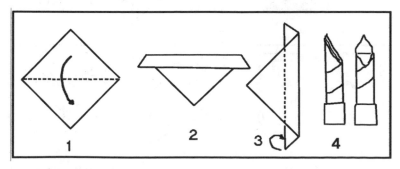

Dedication

To my wonderful and loving Mother

Jeanette Scola. Mom has always been here for us. Raising five boys and one girl was not easy, but mom did a great job! Yes, sometimes she was a bit overbearing and over protective, well she is a mother… What do you expect?

Mom and I have had the opportunity to travel outside the country several times, and I must admit she is a great travel companion. We always stuck together as a family. We always had wonderful meals. Mom and Mama kept complete control in the kitchen, and I mean *control*. The food came to the table like clockwork and WOW was it great. As kids growing up, we never wanted to miss a meal. Mom also made sure we stayed in school and got involved with activities and sports.

Who knows, maybe I can convince my mother to write a book on *How to be a Great Parent*.

PS
Hey, Mom, I'm coming home. Get the pasta and the Italian chicken meatball soup ready!

Michael Scola — I would like to thank my big brother Mike for always being there for me and the whole family. Mike is the "rock" of the family. No matter what the call, Mike will be there to lift you up. And to his very lovely wife Mora who loves to entertain with style, grace and elegance. Mora can and does host the best parties in New Jersey.

PS — Hey, Mike! Remember when I borrowed your new car when I was only 15 years old while you were on vacation with your friends in Seaside Heights? Sorry!

Rosemarie Boos — Rose, as we all call our sister, is without a doubt the best person in the family for communications. We all consult with Rose as to when and where events should and do happen. She was voted the "best sister in the world" by the Scola Brothers.

Raymond Boos is my sister's other half. Always ready to play sports, he is a great father and role model. Glad I have a brother in-law like him. Their son, Joseph, "my nephew," attended school for gifted and talented children and made us proud. Now he is a successful businessman on the East Coast. You go, JOE!

PS — Hey, Rose! Remember that time when we were working on the hot dog truck and got chased out of the park? We took off and left our colorful umbrella up. It snapped in half, and we drove all the way home with it hanging and bouncing off the back of the truck! By the way, did we ever get paid for working?

Alan Scola — Brother Al— Nickname, *Al the Mender.* Alan was my vacation partner. Al and I were the first in the family to travel the world. We were in Europe for…well it was a long time! Al's hobby and love is boating.

Party Planning Secrets

Al's good-looking son Nicky really knows how to charm the ladies.

Terry, Alan's other half, is always ready in a moments notice to go out with Al on his boat.

PS — Hey Alan! Two o'clock you say good morning!

Ricky Scola — Brother Ricky is going about his business raising his talented and beautiful daughter, Ericka. Rick's wife Donna can really cook up a storm.

PS — Hey Ricky, remember the fish you caught at Catalina Island?

Darin Scola — Brother Darin, *the single guy*, loves to operate anything that is big — car crushers, oversized cranes, bulldozers—you name it, he can drive and operate it.

Big Darin and I have had wonderful times traveling outside the country as well.

PS — Hey, Darin, three days and three nights.

Cousin **Dottie Franzmathes**, Thanks for being a part of our family; you're always there for us, and we will always be there for you!

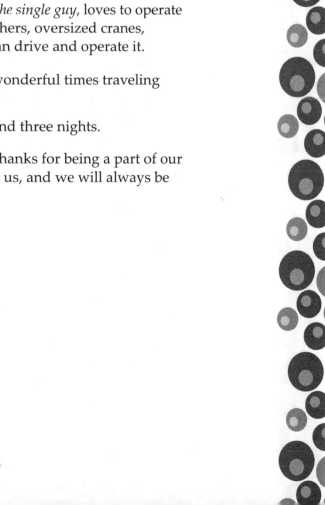

Acknowledgments

Sweetie, My Cat and Best Friend!

Mentors

T. Harv Eker, Peak Potentials Training — After spending three days in a free training seminar offered by Peak Potential, I had enough information and guidance to get myself to the next plateau in life. I decided to sign up for the *Quantum Leap Program* and never looked back. Thanks, Harv, for your wisdom and in believing that we can all achieve our dreams.

Mr. Bob "Bubbie" Koby — He taught me how to be a good human being, and gave me guidance and the opportunity to learn what has happily become my life, the "Food and Beverage Hospitality industry," and to his wonderful wife Rosemary, and family.

Marc Gurvitz — A very special thanks to Marc for giving me friendship, guidance, business opportunities, and, most of all, sobriety. I will always be indebted to him.

Frank Woodward — Businessman, entrepreneur, world-wide caterer, Food Network star, and most of all, friend and teacher. Thanks for your guidance.

Silvia Lowry of A-Packaged Parties — A multi--award-winning party designer who has captured the attention of some of the most prominent people in the world, I have had the pleasure of working with Silvia for many, many years.

I want to thank you for all the knowledge you have bestowed upon me. Our friendship and business relationship will last a lifetime.

Friends Who Helped Me with the Book

George Calfa — Thanks for over 20 years of friendship and helping me with my website, newsletters, recipes and articles—you're the best!

Stephanie Subocz — Thank you for your attention to detail, you really made a difference in the book.

Cousin Nikki Gangemi — Thanks for getting me started.

Ross Weitzberg — Thanks for all your knowledge and valuable time on the edit.

Chef Kyle Mack — You're an amazing teacher with 5-star quality.

Chef Scott E. Logie — Thanks for all of your insight and friendship.

Jack Barnard — Who guided me with the direction of this book.

Lois Smith, Patti Negri, Vivian Lim, Ivette Temesy, Dan Reddington — Thanks for all your input on the book and your friendship over the years.

David Capron, Emotion Portrait Studios — Thank you for all the photos.

My Good Friends Who I Constantly Bounced Ideas Off of

Raymond and Paula Sodeika, Barry, Janea, Mallory and Morgan Marks, Jim, Karen, Stacy and Jennifer Solomos, Mayor Michael Keegan, The Honorable Lynn D. Olson, Rick McConnell, Grady (Sportsman) Mack, Chef Don Tahara and **Ron Byrd.**

Chef Pieps — For giving me the opportunity to be co-star in the TV Show *Recipe for Disaster.*

The **For Stars Catering Gang, Bubba Sienkanic** — Thanks for your friendship and believing in me.

Lloyd Thomas and **Andrea Damiano, Peter and Carrie Starkman, Henri and Maggie Komrij, Silvia Troccoli** — Thanks for being there.

Frank and Michele Woodward — For always being positive and having faith in me (loved you guys on Food Network).

Special Thanks to:

Katti Lippa — One of the most talented and amazing multitaskers I have ever met. Your special skills made this daunting task a pleasure during the most challenging times. You deserve a larger part of the credit in helping me put together one of the best party planning books available for the consumer…I thank you and soon millions will thank you, too.

Barri Sturm — You have been incredible throughout this fun, challenging and rewarding journey. Thank you for your willingness and ability to help organize my thoughts, your dedication to the book, and your patient yet persistend determination to make this the best product of its type on the market. I can't wait to get started on our next project together!

Scott L. Baker — A self-proclaimed "biggest fan of the book," superb lawyer and loyal friend, your input and support have always been under the radar, but always valuable and appreciated. Thank you for your support, reality checks and keeping the energy.

Peter Schankowitz, Videojug US Chief Executive — Thanks for believing in me.

About the Author

*C*harlie Scola is a leading innovator in the food, catering, and party-planning business. Affectionately known as "Party Charlie," he has catered all types of large and small events for major studios, celebrities, rock 'n' roll superstars, political dignitaries, executives, and people who just like to party. His trademark is to provide his clients with a stress-free experience by employing creative, time-tested techniques that maximize the joy of the event while minimizing the cost and virtually eliminating the common mistakes and embarrassments. Charlie has written this book to share ideas and concepts he's gathered for the last 30 years in the hope that you will benefit from his enthusiasm and experience.

Charlie was born in New Jersey in 1956 into what he reminisces was a poor but loving family. Raised by his mother and grandmother, who expertly cooked and baked everything from scratch, Charlie began to learn his trade at an early age. He also learned how food has the power to bring people together. As a young kid in a chaotic household, Charlie realized that meals were the only times when everyone in the family was together, and he looked forward to helping prepare the meals and share in the energy generated by the group.

Party Planning Secrets

Charlie's first paying job at the age of 14 was as a bagel packer at Sonny Amster's Bagels in Union, New Jersey. As soon as he could drive, he teamed up with his brother and sister to form a mobile hotdog vending company peddling New Jersey's Finest Sabrett Hot Dogs and Ma Scola's Best Chili in Town. Ironically, when the truck was purchased, it already had a sign reading Charlie's Hot Dogs painted on the side. It was a sign of an auspicious beginning

When he was 17, Charlie's job moved to New York City, across from Madison Square Garden, where he continued his apprenticeship in a bagel shop, ultimately moving to *Town & Campus Banquet Center*, where he set up the room for parties and worked on other kinds of event preparation. Learning all aspects of event preparation and catering, Charlie was quickly promoted to banquet manager, reporting directly to his mentor, owner Bob "Bubbie" Koby. Charlie credits Bubbie with a "client-first" approach. During his time with Bubbie, Charlie coordinated parties for such impressive figures as Presidents Gerald Ford and Jimmy Carter as well as Nelson Rockefeller. To this day, if you have the opportunity to work with Charlie, you may overhear him say, "Mr. Koby would do it this way." If you didn't hear him say it, you knew he was thinking it.

On Charlie's 23rd birthday, he launched his first banquet facility, called *Exclusively Yours*, which specialized in continental cuisine. Featuring singing waiters and waitresses, *Exclusively Yours* became a favorite hangout for the mayor of Karney, New Jersey, until it was destroyed by a fire in 1980. This devastating event proved to be the motivating force behind Charlie's move to Los Angeles.

Charlie Scola aka PartyCharlie

Charlie honed his catering, design, and party theme skills while working for prominent caterers such as *Luke's Gourmet Catering* and *Rent-a-Yenta*. He built his reputation orchestrating parties for some of the busiest celebrities at the time, including Kenny Rogers, Chuck Norris, and Kim Carnes.

In 1981, Charlie and a colleague, Ileen Anderson, formed a new company appropriately named, *Life's a Party*, which specialized in themed parties and put Charlie on the map as one of L.A.'s premiere caterers and party planners.

An eternal optimist whose philosophy is to share happiness through celebrations, his impressive client list includes such prominent public figures as Jon Lovitz, Tom Shadyak, Eric McCormack, Tom Cruise, J. J. Abrams, Marc Gurvitz, David Spade, Dana Carvey, Bill Maher, Charlie Sheen, John Travolta, Christian Slater, Angela Lansbury, Aaron Spelling, Bruce Springsteen, Elton John, Dolly Parton, Stevie Wonder, Toto, Julio Iglesias, Barry Manilow, Diana Ross, George Strait, Bon Jovi, Rick Dees, Richard Simmons, Hugh Hefner, Pete Rose, Wilt Chamberlain, Senator Ted Kennedy, presidential candidates Bill Bradley and Gary Bauer, Mayor Tom Bradley, State Council Vice Premier of the People's Republic of China, and the Crown Prince of Saudi Arabia.

For over 10 years now, Charlie has been spreading the joy under the moniker *Charlie Scola Catering*, which provides full-service catering, event planning, and consulting. He's handled such events as the grand opening of Universal Studio Hollywood's City Walk for 7000 guests and Hugh Hefner's Millennium and Christmas

Party Planning Secrets

Party at the Playboy mansion. He was recently selected as the official caterer for events held by the City of Beverly Hills, and he's also the Special Events Director of *For Stars Catering*, which goes on location throughout the world and offers food service on film sets, for backstage parties, and for Hollywood's premiere social events. He has put together complete packages for Hollywood premieres.

Currently, Charlie is enjoying speaking and teaching his PartyCharlie secrets in seminars throughout the United States. He has also cracked into showbiz, having appeared on *Bridezilla, Blind Date,* and *Love Connection* and in several commercials. He also did a spot for *People's Court* with the Honorable Mayor Koch. Charlie has held roles in various independent films and even appeared as a Jerry Lewis impersonator live at the famous Jerry Lewis Telethon, much to the delight of the world-renowned comedian himself.

But even with his multitude of successes, Charlie keeps his eye on what is most important to him — God, family, friends, and the joy his business brings to the world. This book is Charlie's way of spreading the joy. Enjoy!

Additional copies of *Party Planning Secrets* are
available through your favorite book dealer
or from the publisher:

Clear Toast Publications
17226 Grevillea Avenue, Suite I
Lawndale, CA 90260
E-mail: info@PartyCharlieBook.com
Website: www.PartyCharlie.com

(ISBN-13: 978-0-9791878-0-3) is $24.95 for
hardbound edition, plus $5.00 shipping for first copy
($2.00 each additional copy)
and sales tax for CA orders.